Adventist Pioneer Classics

The Gospel in Creation

Original Edition

Ellet J. Waggoner

Copyright ©2023
LS COMPANY
ISBN: 978-1-0882-1482-4

Contenido

Introduction 5

Chapter 1—The first day: Creation and Redemption..9

    The Creative Word..10

    The Word, A Sure Foundation 14

    Building On The Word 15

    The Message Of Comfort 19

    "Let There Be Light"..21

    The Light Of Life 23

Chapter 2—The Second Day 28

    Clouds And Showers Of Grace 31

    The Bow Of Promise 33

Chapter 3—The Third Day 35

"Christ In The Tempest" 37

A Lesson From The Grass 39

Chapter 4 — The Fourth Day 47

The Oath Of God 48

God Is A Sun And Shield 49

Grace and Glory 50

Chapter 5 — The Fifth Day 55

Chapter 6 — The Sixth Day 59

Chapter 7 — The Seventh Day 64

Introduction

In the fifteenth chapter of Romans and the fourth verse the Spirit of God, through the Apostle Paul, sets the seal of approval upon the whole of the Old Testament, in giving the object for which it was written. He says, "For whatsoever things were written before were written for our learning, that we through patience and comfort of the Scriptures might have hope."

The reason why we find comfort and hope in the Old Testament is plainly revealed by Christ when, in His reply to the Jews, He gave the Divine sanction to it, and especially to the writings of Moses, saying, "Ye search the Scriptures, because ye think that in them ye have eternal life; and these are they which bear witness of Me." "For if ye believed Moses, ye would believe Me; for he wrote of Me. But if ye believe not his writings, how shall ye believe My words?" John 5:39, 46-47 R.V. We may find comfort and hope in the Scriptures, because Christ is in them.

The spirit of the Old Testament is the Spirit of Christ. We read of the ancient prophets that they searched "what, or what manner of time the Spirit of Christ which was in them did signify, when it testified beforehand the sufferings of Christ, and the glory that should follow." 1 Peter 1:11. Not only so, but the Old Testament contains the Gospel. In the verse following the one last quoted we read, "Unto whom it was revealed, that not unto themselves, but unto us they did minister the things which are now reported unto you by them that have preached the Gospel unto you with the Holy Ghost sent down from heaven." That is, the prophets, Moses among them, ministered the very same things that were preached by the apostles, namely, the Gospel. Since the Gospel of God is "concerning His Son Jesus Christ our Lord," Romans 1:1-3 and the Jews would necessarily have believed in Jesus if they had believed Moses, because Moss wrote of Christ, it follows that what Moses wrote was the Gospel.

The first thing that Moses wrote, through the inspiration of the Spirit of God, was the story of creation. That, therefore, is one of the things through which we are to receive hope and comfort. We can receive hope and comfort through the story of the creation because it contains the Gospel. A few words will serve to establish this fact before we proceed to study the lesson in detail.

The declaration of the apostle, that the Gospel "is the power of God unto salvation to every one that believeth," Romans 1:16 is familiar to all who have ever heard the Gospel preached. The Gospel is the manifestation of God's power put forth to save men. The Apostle Peter states the same thing in substance when he speaks of the inheritance reserved in heaven for those "who are kept by the power of God through faith unto salvation." 1 Peter 1:5

But what is the measure of the power of God? Wherein is it seen in a tangible form? Read Romans 1.20, where we are told that ever since the creation of the world the invisible things of God, even His eternal power and Godhead, are clearly seen, being understood by the things that are made. It is in creation, therefore, that the power of God is to be seen by everybody. But the power of God in the line of salvation is the Gospel. Therefore the works of creation teach the Gospel. This is declared in Psalm 19, where we read, "The heavens declare the glory of God; and the firmament showeth His handiwork. Day unto day uttereth speech, and night unto night showeth knowledge. There is no speech or language; without these their voice is heard. Their line is gone out through all the earth, and their words to the end of the world.

I have given the rendering of the margin, as conforming more closely to the original. The idea is, that no matter what language a people speaks, all can understand the language of the heavens. Their message can be read much more easily than if they uttered an audible sound; for all people on earth cannot understand the same articulate speech, but all who have reason can read the simple language of the works of God.

Addison expresses this thought in the following beautiful lines: -

> "The spacious firmament on high,
>
> With all the blue, ethereal sky,
>
> And spangled heavens, a shining frame,
>
> Their great Original proclaim;
>
> The unwearied sun, from day to day
>
> Does his Creator's power display,
>
> And publishes to every land
>
> The work of an Almighty hand.
>
> "Soon as the evening shades prevail,
>
> The moon takes up the wondrous tale;

> And nightly, to the listening earth
> Repeats the story of her birth;
> While all the stars that round her burn,
> And all the planets in their turn,
> Confirm the tidings as they roll,
> And spread the truth from pole to pole.
> "What though in solemn silence, all
> Move round the dark terrestrial ball?
> What though no real voice nor sound
> Amid their radiant orbs be found?
> In reason's ear they all rejoice,
> And utter forth a glorious voice,
> For ever singing, as they shine,
> 'The hand that made us is Divine.'"

The Gospel is the power of God, and the power of God is manifest in the things that He has made; therefore the Psalmist is speaking of the Gospel, which the heavens teach.

The Apostle Paul in Romans 10:15-18 shows that this is so, "How beautiful are the feet of them that preach the gospel of peace, and bring glad tidings of good things! But they have not all obeyed the gospel. For Isaiah says, Lord, who has believed our report? So then faith comes by hearing, and hearing by the word of God. But I say, have they not heard? Yes verily, their sound went into all the earth, and their words unto the ends of the world." The apostle is here speaking about the Gospel, which, he says, all have not obeyed. Then he declares that all have heard, and as proof that they have all heard he quotes from Psalm 19, "Their line is gone out through all the earth, and their words to the end of the world." Their words concerning what? Why, concerning the Gospel, of course. Thus we have a plain statement that the heavens do preach the Gospel. There is no man so illiterate that he cannot read the Gospel; no man so deaf or so isolated that he cannot hear a gospel sermon. This truth will be more evident as we proceed.

Chapter 1—The first day: Creation and Redemption

"In the beginning God created the heaven and the earth." Genesis 1.1

In this brief sentence we have the whole of the truth of the Gospel summed up. He who reads aright may derive a world of comfort from it. In the first place, let us consider who it was that created the heaven and the earth. "God created." But Christ is God, the brightness of the Father's glory, and the express image of His person. Hebrews 1.3. He Himself said, "I and My Father are one." John 10.30. He it was who, representing the Father, created the heaven and the earth. "In the beginning was the Word, and the Word was with God, and the Word was God. The same was in the beginning with God. All things were made by Him; and without Him was not anything made that was made." John 1.1-3. And again we read of Christ, that "by Him were all things created, that are in heaven, and that are in earth, visible and invisible, whether they be thrones, or dominions, or principalities, or powers: all things were created by Him and for Him: and He is before all things, and by Him all things consist." Colossians 1.16,17. The Father Himself addresses the Son as God and as Creator. The first chapter of Hebrews says that God has not at any time said to any of the angels, "Thou art My Son, this day have I begotten Thee." "But unto the Son He saith, Thy throne, O God, is for ever and ever: a sceptre of righteousness is the sceptre of Thy kingdom." And He has also said to the Son, "Thou, Lord, in the beginning hast laid the foundation of the earth, and the heavens are the works of Thine hands." Hebrews 1.5,8,10. So we are well assured that when we read in the first chapter of Genesis, "In the beginning God created the heaven and the earth," it refers to God in Christ.

Creative power is the distinguishing mark of Divinity. The Spirit of the Lord, through the prophet Jeremiah, describes the vanity of idols, and then continues, "But the Lord is the true God, He is the living God, and an everlasting King: at His wrath the earth shall tremble, and the nations shall not be able to abide His indignation. Thus shall ye say unto them, the gods that have not made the heavens and the earth, even they shall perish from the earth, and from under these heavens. He hath made the earth by His power, He hath established the world by His wisdom, and hath stretched out the heavens by His discretion." Jeremiah 10.10-12. The earth was made by His power, and established by His Wisdom. But Christ is "the power of God, and the wisdom of God." So here again we find Christ inseparably connected with creation as the Creator. Only as we acknowledge and worship Christ as the Creator do we acknowledge His Divinity.

Christ is Redeemer by virtue of His power as Creator. We read, "We have redemption through His blood, even the forgiveness of sins," because that "by Him were all things created." Colossians 1.14,16. If He were not Creator, He could not be Redeemer.

This means simply that redemptive power and creative power are the same. To redeem is to create. This is shown in the statement of the apostle that the Gospel is the power of God unto salvation and this power is the power of God as is seen by means of the things that He has been made. Romans 1.16,20. When we consider the works of creation, and think of the power manifested in them, we are contemplating the power of redemption.

There has been a great deal of idle speculation as to which is the greater, redemption or creation. Many have thought that redemption is a greater work than creation. Such speculation is idle, because only infinite power could perform either work, and infinite power cannot be measured by human minds. But while we cannot measure the power, we can easily settle the question of which is the greater, because the Scriptures give us the information. Neither is greater than the other, for both are the same. Redemption is creation. Redemption is the same power that was put forth in the beginning to create the world and all that is in it, now put forth to save men and the earth from the curse of sin.

The Scriptures are very clear on this point. The Psalmist prayed, "Create in me a clean heart, and renew a right spirit within me." Psalms 51.10. The apostle says, that "if any man be in Christ, he is a new creature," 2 Corinthians 5.17 or a new creation. And again we read, "For by grace are ye saved through faith; and that not of yourselves: it is the gift of God: not of works, lest any man should boast. For we are His workmanship, created in Christ Jesus unto good works, which God hath before ordained, that we should walk in them." Ephesians 2.8-10.

Compared with God, man is "less than nothing, and vanity." Isaiah 40.17. In him "dwelleth no good thing." Romans 7.18. Now the same power that in the beginning made the earth from nothing, takes man, if he is willing, and makes of him that which is "to the praise of the glory of His grace." Ephesians 1:6.

The Creative Word

Having seen that Christ, the Word, is the Creator of all things, and that He redeems by His creative power, let us now learn what the Bible says as to how He created. Here is the answer: "By the word of the Lord were the heavens made; and all the host of them by the breath of His mouth. He gathereth the waters of the sea together as a heap: He lays up the depth in storehouses. Let all the earth fear the Lord: let all the inhabitants of the world stand in awe of Him. For He spake, and it was; He commanded, and it stood fast." Psalms 33.6-9. It is very simple, and most wonderful because of its very simplicity. Well may we all exclaim, "What a word is this!"

"Through faith we understand that the worlds were framed by the word of God, so that things which are seen were not made of things which do appear." Hebrews 11.3. How do we know how the worlds were made? By faith. Faith gives knowledge. That is its special work. Knowledge gained by faith is not vague and uncertain, but is the most absolutely certain of any knowledge. In fact, there is no real knowledge that does not spring from faith. Knowledge that comes in any other way is speculation. The unbelieving soul regards faith as folly, but the faithful soul knows that faith makes for it a solid foundation. Whoever will believe may know.

The knowledge of the alphabet is one of the most common things in the world. It lies at the very foundation of all learning. No one ridicules the child saying that he knows the letters of the alphabet, and for declaring most positively, in spite of all contradiction, that "A" is "A". And yet he knows that only by faith. He has never investigated the subject for himself; he has accepted the statement of his teacher. The teacher himself had to learn the alphabet in the same way - by faith. It was not demonstrated to him that "A" is "A." It could not have been. If he had refused to believe the fact till it was demonstrated to him, he never would have learned to read. He had to accept the fact by faith, and then it would prove itself true under every circumstance. There is nothing of which people are more absolutely sure than they are of the letters of the alphabet, and there is nothing for which they are more absolutely dependent on faith.

Now, just as the child learns the alphabet, so we learn the truths of God. Whoever receives the kingdom of heaven must receive it as a little child. By faith we learn to know Jesus Christ, who is the Alpha and the Omega, - the entire alphabet of God. He who believes the simple statement of the Bible, concerning creation, may know for a certainty that God did create the heaven and the earth by the power of His Word. The fact that some unbeliever doubts this, and thinks it is foolish, does not shake his knowledge, nor prove that he does not know it, any more than our knowledge of the alphabet is shaken or disproved by some other person's ignorance of it.

"By the word of the Lord were the heavens made; and all the host of them by the breath of His mouth." In the Century Magazine of May 1891, there was a very interesting description of the production of voice-figures. The article was entitled "Visible Sound." Mrs. Watts Hughes had employed a simple device to test the intensities of vocal sounds. It was an elastic membrane stretched over the mouth of a receiver, into which receiver the voice was introduced by means of a wide mouthed tube. On this membrane sand or fine powder was sprinkled. It was found that upon singing into the tube the powder was gently agitated by the vibrations of the membrane, which vibrations correspond to those of the voice, differing according to the pitch and intensity of the sound. This, of course, was what might be expected. But the wonder was that in every instance the agitation produced the shape of some plant or flower, or even of some of the lower forms of animal life. Something similar to this may be seen when one breathes upon the windowpane in frosty weather.

It was found that when the powder was dry it would not retain the form after the vibration of the voice ceased. So the expedient was adopted of slightly moistening it, when the various shapes could be retained and photographed.

This shows that the breath, as it comes from the lungs, has the shape of living things, and to the singer suggested a thought, which she thus expresses: -

"Closing now my brief sketch of these voice-figures, as I have observed them, I would add that my experiments have been made as a vocalist, using my own voice as the instrument of investigation; and I must leave it for others more acquainted with natural science to adjust the accordance of the these appearances with facts and laws already known. Yet, passing from one stage to another of these inquiries, question after question has presented itself to me, until I have continually felt myself standing before mystery, in great part hidden, although some glimpses seem revealed. And I must say, besides, that as day by day I have gone on singing into shape these peculiar forms, and, stepping out of doors, have seen their parallels living in the flowers, ferns, and trees around me; and, again, as I have watched the little heaps in the formation of the floral figures gather themselves up, and then shoot out their petals, just as a flower springs form the swollen bud - the hope has come to me that these humble experiments may afford some suggestions in regard to Nature's production of her own beautiful forms, and may thereby aid, in some slight degree, the revelation of yet another link in the great chain of the organized universe that, we are told in Holy Writ, took its shape at the voice of God."

This is not given as an example of how the Lord spoke the earth into existence in the beginning, for we cannot know how He did it, but it will serve to help us to grasp the fact. Man is made in the image of God, but he has no creative power. In his breath there can be only the forms of living things; but in the breath of God there are not only the forms, but the very living things themselves, for He is the living God, and with Him is "the fountain of life." When He speaks, the word, which names the thing, contains the very thing itself. Whatever the word describes exists in living form in that word.

This is indicated by the words of the Apostle Paul concerning God that He "calleth those things which be not as though they were." This is an attribute of Divinity alone. If a man calls a thing that is not, as though it were, it is a lie. But God does so, and He cannot lie. How is this? Simply because that when He calls a thing by name, or says that a thing will be, it already exists, even though it cannot be seen. The thing is in His word. When He names a thing that previously had no existence, that instant the thing exists, for His word forms it as He names it. When He says that a thing will be, and then it is as sure as though it had already appeared, because it does really exist in the word that has been spoken. It is for this reason that so much of prophecy is in the perfect tense, as though already accomplished. So when the worlds were to be brought into existence, God spoke, and there they were. The breath of His mouth formed them.

Now see how firm a foundation is given the believing one who knows that all things were created by the word of God, and that when God speaks the thing named exists, full of life. The Psalmist says, "I will hear what God the Lord will speak: for He will speak peace unto His people, and to His saints." Psalms 85.8. He speaks peace through the Divine Word, "for He is our peace." Ephesians 2.14. But peace means righteousness, for we read, "Great peace have they which love Thy law: and nothing shall offend them," (Psalms 119.165) or cause them to stumble. And again, "O that thou hadst hearkened to My commandments! then had thy peace been as a river, and thy righteousness as the waves of the sea." Isaiah 48.18. Then it must be that God speaks righteousness when He speaks peace. And so it is, for again we read: -

"But now the righteousness of God without the law is manifested, being witnessed by the law and the prophets; even the righteousness of God which is by faith of Jesus Christ unto all and upon all them that believe: for there is no difference: for all have sinned, and come short of the glory of God; being justified (made righteous, or doers of the law) freely by His grace through the redemption that is in Christ Jesus: whom God hath set forth to be a propitiation through faith in His blood, to declare His righteousness for the remission of sins that are past, through the forbearance of God; to declare, I say, at this time His righteousness: that He might be just, and the Justifier of Him which believeth in Jesus." Romans 3.21-26.

Notice that man is declared to have no righteousness: "There is none that doeth good, no, not one." Romans 3.12. No one has anything in him out of which righteousness can be made. Then the righteousness of God is put, literally, into and upon all that believe. Then they are both clothed with righteousness, and filled with it, according to the Scripture. In fact, they then become "the righteousness of God" in Christ. And how is this accomplished? God declares His righteousness upon the one who believes. To declare is to speak. So God speaks to the sinner, who is nothing, and who has nothing, and says, "You are righteous," and immediately that believing sinner ceases to be a sinner, and is the righteousness of God. The word of God which speaks righteousness has the righteousness itself in it, and as soon as the sinner believes, and receives that word into his own heart by faith, that moment he has the righteousness of God in his heart; and since out of the heart are the issues of life, it follows that a new life is thus begun in him; and that life is a life of obedience to the commandments of God. Thus faith is indeed the substance of things hoped for, because faith appropriates the word of God, and the word of God is substance.

The Word, A Sure Foundation

The same word that created the earth also upholds it. We quote again the words concerning Christ: "For in Him were all things created, in the heavens and upon the earth, things visible and things invisible, whether thrones or dominions or principalities or powers; all things have been created through Him, and unto Him; and He is before all things, and in Him all things consist." Colossians 1.16,17. To consist means to hold together. Therefore all things on the earth, and the earth itself, owe their continued existence to Christ. So Paul declared on Mars' Hill, "In Him we live, and move, and have our being." Acts 17.28

This upholding is by His word. Thus: "God, who at sundry times and in divers manners spake in time past unto the fathers by the prophets, hath in these last days spoken unto us by His Son, whom He hath appointed heir of all things, by whom also He made the worlds; who being the brightness of His glory, and the express image of His person, and upholding all things by the word of His power, when He had by Himself purged our sins, sat down on the right hand of the Majesty on high." Hebrews 1.1-3. Christ is the Divine Word; He is in the spoken word; and so, since all things hold together in Him, they are upheld by His powerful word.

Read also the words written by the Apostle Peter: "By the word of God the heavens were of old, and the earth standing out of the water and in the water: whereby the world that then was, being overflowed with water, perished: but the heavens and the earth, which are now, by the same word are kept in store, reserved unto fire against the day of judgment and perdition of ungodly men." 2 Peter 3.5-7. The same word that made the earth caused its overflow by a flood, brought it transformed from the waters, and still upholds it. That word, therefore, must indeed be substantial. It is more real and solid than the earth itself, even as the foundation of a thing must be more substantial than the thing. That word "liveth and abideth for ever." 1 Peter 1.23. Therefore the one who trusts it will never be at a loss.

There will come a time when "the earth shall reel to and fro like a drunkard, and shall be removed like a cottage"; (Isaiah 24.19,20) when every island shall flee away, and "the mountains be carried into the midst of the sea." But even in that awful time the Christian can say, "God is our refuge and strength, a very present help in trouble. Therefore will not we fear." Psalms 46.1,2

Building On The Word

"Therefore whosoever heareth these sayings of Mine, and doeth them, I will liken him unto a wise man, which built his house upon a rock: and the rain descended, and the floods came, and the winds blew, and beat upon that house; and it fell not: for it was founded upon a rock. And every one that heareth these sayings of Mine, and doeth them not, shall be likened unto a foolish man, which built his house upon the sand: and the rain descended, and the floods came, and the winds blew, and beat upon that house; and it fell; and great was the fall of it." Matthew 7.24-27.

Christ is a rock. Of the ancient Israelites we read, "they drank of that spiritual Rock that followed (went with) them; and that Rock was Christ." 1 Corinthians 10.4. The Psalmist says, "He is my rock, and there is no unrighteousness in Him." Psalms 92.15. To those who take Him as their peace, it is said: "Now therefore ye are no more strangers and foreigners, but fellow-citizens with the saints, and of the household of God; and are built upon the foundation of the apostles and prophets, Jesus Christ Himself being the chief corner stone." Ephesians 2.19,20. We are not built upon the apostles and prophets, but upon the foundation, which they have built upon; "for other foundation can no man lay than that is laid, which is Jesus Christ." 1 Corinthians 3:11.

According to the words of Christ, in the Sermon on the Mount, we build upon the rock by hearing and doing His words. The word of God is "God breathed," and therefore full of His own life. "Faith cometh by hearing, and hearing by the word of God," (Romans 10.17) and Christ dwells in the heart by faith; therefore the word has Christ in it, because it brings Christ into the heart. The word of a man stands for the man himself. It is worth just as much as he is. If he is a worthless character, his word is worth nothing; but if he is an honorable man, and has promised a thing, his word is worth all that he is worth, or all that he can do. The word represents him. We say that a man does a thing, which his servant does in obedience to his word. So the word of God stands for Himself. All that God is worth, His word is worth. It represents Him, because it is full of His life.

Abraham is a wonderful example of building on Christ by believing His word. God made a promise to Abraham, which, like all the promises of God, was in Christ. Then the record says of Abraham, "And he believed in the Lord; and He counted it to him for righteousness." Genesis 15.6. There is something very peculiar about this expression "he believed in the Lord." The word rendered "believed" is from the Hebrew word "Amen." In the word "Amen" we have as nearly as possible the exact form of the Hebrew. The word is not translated, but simply transferred. It is a Hebrew word, and appears in the and the floods came, and the winds blew, and beat upon that house; and it fell not: for it was founded upon a rock. And every one that heareth these sayings of Mine, and doeth them not, shall be likened unto a foolish man, which built his house upon the sand: and the rain descended, and the floods came, and the winds blew, and beat upon that house; and it fell; and great was the fall of it." Matthew 7.24-27

The root idea of the word is firmness. The idea of solidity and stability attaches to it. It has a variety of definitions, all carrying this thought. One definition is "to build, or depend, on." So, literally, Abraham built upon God, and it was counted unto him for righteousness. This agrees with the idea that the word of the Lord is a foundation. The root idea of the word being that of something substantial, upon which one can build, is carried into our ordinary speech. We say of a certain man, "You can depend on his word." That means that you can rest your weight upon it. Now if this be true of a man, how much more so of God! We may rest upon His word, for it will always hold us up.

This gives a better idea of the Bible meaning of belief than is commonly held. People generally think that to believe is nothing more than to nod assent. But believing the Lord is much more than this. It is to count that word as the surest thing in the universe, since it is that which upholds the universe, and to rest the whole soul, and all the hopes, upon it, even though everything appears contrary to it. It is to walk where there seems to be nothing, provided the word of the Lord is there, knowing that it is a firm foundation. The poet Whittier has thus expressed it: -

> "Nothing before, nothing behind;
>
> The steps of faith
>
> Fall on the seeming void, and find

The rock beneath."

When the Lord said to Peter "Come," as He walked on the water, Peter got out of the boat and started to his Lord. It is contrary to nature for a man to walk on the water. It is impossible that water should hold a man up. What did hold Peter up? It was that word "Come." When the Lord utters a word, the thing described is in the word; and so when he said to Peter "Come," the power to come was in the word. It was on that that Peter walked as long as he walked at all. When he looked around him at the boisterous waves he began to sink. Why? Because he then forgot the word, and thought only of the water. As soon as he left the word he began to sink, because the water had no power to hold him up. It was only the word of the Lord that could keep him above the water. If the word of the Lord had told Peter to walk in the air, he could have done that just as easily as he could have walked on the water. The word of the Lord bore Elijah through the air, and so it will soon do for all who learn the power of it.

But note the fact, that when Abraham built on the Lord it was counted to him for righteousness. The Lord never makes any mistakes in His reckoning. When Abraham's faith was reckoned to him for righteousness, it was because it was indeed righteousness. How so? Why, as Abraham built on God, he built on everlasting righteousness. "He is my rock, and there is no unrighteousness in Him." He became one with the Lord, and so God's righteousness was his own.

"The words of the Lord are pure words: as silver tried in a furnace of earth, purified seven times." Psalms 12.6. Therefore he who builds upon the Rock Jesus Christ, by accepting His word in living faith, builds upon a tried foundation. So we read: "Wherefore laying aside all malice, and all guile, and hypocrisies, and envies, and all evil speaking, as newborn babes, desire the sincere milk of the word, that ye may grow thereby: if so be ye have tasted that the Lord is gracious. To whom coming, as unto a living stone, disallowed indeed of men, but chosen of God, and precious, ye also, as lively stones, are built up a spiritual house, an holy priesthood, to offer up spiritual sacrifices, acceptable to God by Jesus Christ. Wherefore also it is contained in the Scripture, Behold, I lay in Zion a chief corner stone, elect, precious: and he that believeth on him shall not be confounded." 1 Peter 2.1-6.

The force of this is not so clearly seen until we read the passage of Scripture, which is quoted by the apostle, in connection with the one that we have quoted from the Saviour's Sermon on the Mount. Recalling the latter, we read from the prophecy of Isaiah: -

"Therefore thus saith the Lord God, Behold, I lay in Zion for a foundation a stone, a tried stone, a precious corner-stone of sure foundation: he that believeth shall not make haste.

And I will make judgment the line, and righteousness the plummet: and the hail shall sweep away the refuge of lies, and the waters shall overflow the hiding place. And your covenant with death shall be disannulled, and your agreement with hell shall not stand; when the overflowing scourge shall pass through, then ye shall be trodden down by it. As often as it passeth through, it shall take you; for morning by morning shall it pass through, by day and by night: and it shall be nought but terror to understand the message." Isaiah 28.16

Christ is the tried foundation. Righteousness is the plummet by which He is laid. His character is perfectly true and right. Satan exhausted all his arts in trying to lead Him to sin, and was unsuccessful. He is a sure foundation. We build on Him by believing His word, as He Himself said. The floods will surely come. There will be an overflowing scourge that will sweep away the refuge of lies, and all who have built on a false foundation. The house built on the sand will certainly fall. When the storm begins to beat with fury, those who have made lies their refuge will flee for their lives as their foundation begins to totter; but the flood will carry them away. This is the picture presented by the two passages of Scripture.

But far different will it be with those who have built on the Rock of Ages. That sure foundation will stand every blast. Nothing can shake it. Those who have built on it will not make haste. They have often proved that it is a sure refuge, and so they can calmly watch the torrent. They do not need to flee for their lives. Having built on the rock, they are as secure as the rock itself. And why? Because they are really a part of the Rock, for -all who build upon it. Listen to the words of the apostle: "And now, brethren, I commend you to God, and to the word of His grace, which is able to build you up, and to give you an inheritance among all them which are sanctified." Acts 20.32. When one builds upon the Rock, the Rock itself, being a living Rock, grows up into them, so that the foundation and the building are all one piece. This is shown by many passages of Scripture. We will repeat a few.

"For both He that sanctifieth and they who are sanctified are all of one: for which cause He is not ashamed to call them brethren." Hebrews 2:11.

"Now therefore ye are no more strangers and foreigners, but fellow-citizens with the saints, and of the household of God; and are built upon the foundation of the apostles and prophets, Jesus Christ Himself being the chief corner stone; in whom all the building fitly framed together groweth unto an holy temple in the Lord: in whom ye also are builded together for an habitation of God through the Spirit." Ephesians 2.19-22.

"To whom coming, as unto a living stone, disallowed indeed of men, but chosen of God, and precious, ye also, as lively stones, are built up a spiritual house." 1 Peter 2:4-5.

"As ye have therefore received Christ Jesus the Lord, so walk ye in Him: rooted and built up in Him, and established in the faith." Colossians 2:6-7.

Here we have combined the figure of a house with that of a plant. This is perfectly natural, because the Rock upon which we build is a living stone, and gives life to those who are built upon it, so that they, as lively stones, grow into a building. The Apostle Paul combines the two figures: "Ye are God's husbandry, ye are God's building." 1 Corinthians 3:9.

This is also shown very beautifully in the exhortation, which Jehoshaphat gave to Israel when at the command of the Lord they were going out against a vastly superior force, trusting in His word that He would fight for them. "And they rose early in the morning, and went forth into the wilderness of Tekoa: and as they went forth, Jehoshaphat stood and said, "Hear me, O Judah, and ye inhabitants of Jerusalem; Believe in the Lord your God, so shall ye be established; believe His prophets, so shall ye prosper." 2 Chronicles 20.20. Here, as we have seen in the cast of Abraham, the word "believe" is from the Hebrew word "Amen." The word "established" is also another form of the very same word. So that the passage might properly be rendered thus: "Build upon the Lord your God, so shall ye be built up."

The Message Of Comfort

One more point only will be given to show the hope and comfort that are contained in the things that were written aforetime. The fortieth chapter of Isaiah is wholly a message of comfort.

It begins, "Comfort ye, comfort ye My people, saith your God." Then follows an assurance of forgiveness, and then the special message is given by the voice of one crying in the wilderness. That message is the power of the word of God, as contrasted with the weakness of man. "The voice said, Cry. And he said, What shall I cry? All flesh is grass, and all the goodliness thereof is as the flower of the field: the grass withereth, the flower fadeth: because the Spirit of the Lord bloweth upon it: surely the people is grass. The grass withereth, the flower fadeth: but the word of our God shall stand for ever." Isaiah 40.1-8.

Then follow illustrations of the power of the word. The facts of creation are referred to, and the power of God is contrasted with the weakness of men. Then comes this beautiful passage: "To whom then will ye liken Me, that I should be equal to him? Saith the Holy One. Lift up your eyes on high, and see who hath created these, that bringeth out their host by number: He calleth them all by name; by the greatness of His might, and for that He is strong in power, not one is lacking." Isaiah 40:25-26.

Here again we are referred to the fact that God is the upholder of the heavens; that it is His power that keeps the heavenly bodies in their places. But for His direct interposition there would be chaos. In the following verses this fact is offered to the people of God for their special encouragement. "Why sayest thou, O Jacob, and speakest, O Israel, My way is hid from the Lord, and my judgment is passed over from my God? Have you not known? Have you not heard, that the everlasting God, the Lord, the Creator of the ends of the earth, fainteth not, neither is weary? There is no searching of His understanding. He giveth power to the faint; and to them that have no might He increaseth strength." Isaiah 40:27-29.

What a lesson of trust is here! "God hath spoken once; twice have I heard this; that power belongeth unto God." Psalms 62.11. That power is the power that upholds the heavens, and causes the stars and planets to hold their courses. It is this power that He gives to the faint, and to those who have no might, if they will but trust Him. Let a despondent soul but spend a little time in contemplation of the heavens, thinking the while of this passage, and he will be better able than ever before to realize what the apostle means when he says, "Strengthened with all might, according to His glorious power, unto all patience and longsuffering, with joyfulness." Colossians 1:11.

But what is all this intended to show? The power of the word, for it is by the word of His power that all things are upheld. It is the word of the Lord that has created all things. That word is brought to our attention in the first part of the chapter, in contrast with all flesh, as the word that abideth forever. Read now the fortieth chapter of Isaiah entire, especially verses 6 - 8, and 26, and then read the Apostle Peter's comment: -

"Being born again, not of corruptible seed, but of incorruptible, by the word of God, which liveth and abideth for ever. For all flesh is as grass, and all the glory of man as the flower of grass. The grass withereth, and the flower thereof falleth away: but the word of the Lord endureth for ever." 1 Peter 1.23-25. Here we have the quotation from the fortieth of Isaiah concerning the word of God, which creates and upholds all things. It is the living word, which is the life and strength of all things. Take this all in, and then read the closing words of the apostle: "And this is the word which by the gospel is preached unto you."

The Gospel, then, is simply the creative power of God applied to men. Any gospel that leaves creation out, or which does not preach the creative power of God, as seen in the things that He has made, and which does not comfort men by that power, calling upon them ever to keep it in mind as their only source of strength, is "another gospel," which is simply no gospel at all, since there can be no other.

This, then, is the lesson to be learned "in the beginning." He who has learned it is a new creature in Christ, and is ready to learn that which follows, namely, the lesson of growth. With these wonderful facts in mind, how worse than useless do the fears seem which some express: "I am afraid that if I begin the Christian life I shall not be able to hold out." Of course, you wouldn't be able to hold out. You are without strength; but help has been laid upon One that is mighty. He is able to make you stand, and to keep you to the end. "Kept by the power of God through faith unto salvation ready to be revealed in the last time." Therefore,

"Now unto Him that is able to keep you from falling, and to present you faultless before the presence of His glory with exceeding joy, to the only wise God our Saviour, be glory and majesty, dominion and power, both now and ever. Amen." Jude 24, 25.

"Let There Be Light"

"And God said, "Let there be light": and there was light. And God saw the light, that it was good: and God divided the light from the darkness." Genesis 1:3-4.

Hitherto there had been darkness upon the face of the abyss. It was not such darkness as we are accustomed to; for in the thickest darkness man has ever known since that time (with the possible exception of the plague of darkness in Egypt) there has been some mixture of light. Some light tempers the darkness, even in the black night when neither moon nor stars appear; but here there was darkness such as man cannot conceive of, for light had not yet been created.

Out of this thick darkness God commanded the light to shine. The apostle tells us that God "commanded the light to shine out of darkness." 2 Corinthians 4:6.

Here again we are brought to see the wonder of creative power. God does not work as man does. Man has to have the material all ready to his hand when he makes a thing. God is not limited in that way. Utter nothingness is as suitable for His purpose as anything can be. "God hath chosen the foolish things of the world to confound the wise; and God hath chosen the weak things of the world to confound the things which are mighty; and base things of the world, and things which are despised, hath God chosen, yea, and things which are not, to bring to nought things that are: that no flesh should glory in His presence." 1 Corinthians 1:27-29. This is done for our sakes, that we may learn to put our trust in Him.

So when God would make the light, He caused it to shine out of the darkness. Shall we say that He made the light out of the darkness? It would not be improper, for that is in God's power. "If I say, "Surely the darkness shall cover me; even the night shall be light about me. Yea, the darkness hides not from Thee; but the night shineth as the day: the darkness and the light are both alike to Thee." Psalms 139.11,12. And in speaking for the comfort of His people in time of trouble God says: "I will bring the blind by a way that they knew not; I will lead them in paths that they have not known: I will make darkness light before them, and crooked things straight. These things will I do unto them, and not forsake them." Isaiah 42:16

Nothing is too hard for the Lord. He Himself is the Source of all things. The wise soul sees God in all His works. He has impressed Himself upon all creation. It is all stamped with His own personality. The gross darkness of the heathen came from perverting this truth. Instead of seeing the power of God in everything, they said that everything is God. Thus they turned the truth of God into a lie. But it is a fact that from God Himself everything springs. So God could make light shine out of the darkness, because He Himself is light. "This then is the message which we have heard of Him, and declare unto you, that God is light, and in Him is no darkness at all." 1 John 1:5.

Let us not forget, as we study creation, that Christ is the Creator. He is the wisdom of God and the power of God. He it was that created light. He made it from Himself, for in Him are all things created. It is not alone in the spiritual sense that Christ is the Light of the world. The light that rejoices the eyes of all mankind is light that is shed on them from Christ. The visible is to teach us of the invisible. From the natural we are to learn of the spiritual. The physical light that shines in the world is designed to teach us that God is light, and that spiritual light from Him shines as freely for all, and is none the less real. "Unto the upright there ariseth light in the darkness," (Psalms 112:4) so that he may say, "Rejoice not against me, O mine enemy: when I fall, I shall arise; when I sit in darkness, the Lord shall be a light unto me." Micah 7:8.

Christ is the Light of the world. So we read, that when He went into Galilee the words of the prophet concerning that region were fulfilled: "The land of Zebulun, and the land of Naphtali, toward the sea, beyond Jordan, Galilee of the Gentiles; the people which sat in darkness saw a great light, and to them which sat in the region and shadow of death, to them did light spring up." Matthew 4:15-16. Sin is darkness, and it brings darkness

The word of the Lord is light; but that was virtually hidden from the people when the Lord came to earth. Men wise in their own conceit had taken upon themselves the "interpretation" of the law of God, and, as a consequence, had covered it up. They had taken away the key of knowledge. Even thus it was in the Middle Ages, which are generally known as the Dark Ages, for then the Bible was a proscribed book. It was imprisoned in the dark cell, and its rays did not enlighten the people. Men groped for light, and did not know which way to go. The knowledge of God well nigh departed from the land; for even the priests, whose lips should keep knowledge, were ignorant of the Living Oracles. Satan had caused false ideas of God and the right to prevail.

It was into such a state of darkness that Christ, the Light of the world, came. To them that sat in darkness, light sprang up. The light shone in the darkness, and the darkness did not apprehend or overcome it. Nothing could quench that holy, living Light. When men groped in darkness, and knew not the way of truth, the light of Christ's life shone forth in the darkness, to show them the way. All this the aged Simeon saw when he took the Infant Jesus in his arms, and said, "Mine eyes have seen Thy salvation, which Thou hast prepared before the face of all people; a light to lighten the Gentiles, and the glory of Thy people Israel." Luke 2:30-32.

The Light Of Life

As sin is darkness, so it is death. "By one man sin entered into the world, and death by sin; and so death passed upon all men, for that all have sinned." Romans 5.12. "For to be carnally minded is death." Romans 8.6. "Sin, when it is full grown, bringeth forth death" (James 1.15); for "the sting of death is sin." 1 Corinthians 15.56. Sin and death come from Satan, for it is he that has the power of death. Therefore it is that we are told that we wrestle not with flesh and blood, but with the rulers of the darkness of this world. The darkness of this world is the darkness of sin, and that is the darkness of the shadow of death. Those who sit in sin sit in the shadow of death; and the light that springs up to such is the light of Christ's sinless life.

As sin is death, so righteousness is life. "To be spiritually minded is life." To be spiritually minded is to have the mind of the Spirit of God; and that is to have His life and righteousness. It is to have the law of God in the mind, "for we know that the law is spiritual." The only thing that can dispel darkness is light. So the only thing that can take away sin is righteousness. And the only thing that can overcome death is life.

The life of man cannot gain the victory over death, for it is death itself. Sin is natural to the heart of mankind. "For from within, out of the heart of men, proceed evil thoughts, adulteries, fornications, murders, thefts, covetousness, wickedness, deceit, lasciviousness, an evil eye, blasphemy, pride, foolishness: all these evil things come from within, and defile the man." Mark 7.21-23. But the heart is the seat of life, "for out of it are the issues of life." Proverbs 4.3. Therefore, since sin is death, and sin in all its various forms springs from the heart, it follows that the very source of man's life is poisoned with death. The life of man is but a living death. The Apostle Paul, after bemoaning the utter sinfulness of the natural man, cried out, "O wretched man that I am! Who shall deliver me from this body of death?" Romans 7:24.

Since righteousness, and that alone, is life, man can have no hope of life from himself, for he can get no righteousness from himself. "A good man out of the good treasure of his heart bringeth forth that which is good; and an evil man out of the evil treasure of his heart bringeth forth that which is evil." Luke 6.45. Man has only evil in his heart by nature; therefore he can bring forth only that which is evil. The Scriptures give abundant witness to this. Let them tell their own story.

"All have sinned, and come short of the glory of God." Romans 3.23. "They are all gone out of the way, they are together become unprofitable; there is none that doeth good, no, not one." Romans 3.12. "Because the carnal mind is enmity against God: for it is not subject to the law of God, neither indeed can be. So then they that are in the flesh cannot please God." Romans 8.7,8. No matter how much the awakened soul may wish that he could do what he knows is right, he has no power in himself to do it. "For the flesh lusteth against the spirit, and the spirit against the flesh: and these are contrary the one to the other: so that ye cannot do the things that ye would." Galatians 5:17.

Now, since only evil can come from evil, and the heart of man brings forth only evil, it is a denial of the Scripture to claim that man can of himself do any good thing. First, because the Bible says that he cannot. Second, whoever says that there is any power in man to do that, which is good, thereby denies that there is any such thing as evil in man. For there cannot be some evil and some good in man by nature. A fountain cannot send forth from the same opening both sweet water and bitter. A little poisonous water will taint the entire fountain. "A little leaven leaveneth the whole lump." 1 Corinthians 5.6. So, if there is any evil in a man by nature, he must be, as the Scripture says, wholly evil. Therefore it is, that whoever says that he can of himself do any good thing, however small, denies that there is any trace of evil in him. But Christ has told the truth about man in the words, "Apart from Me ye can do nothing." John 15:5 R.V.

Third, there is one other possible position for the one who says that he can of himself do that which is good, and that is to claim that he can make good out of evil. There are many who openly claim that evil is only "undeveloped good"; but they do not any more strongly assert that claim than do those who think that they are able of themselves to do that which is good. To say that evil is undeveloped good is to deny the Bible, which says that man has no good thing in him. And to intimate that sin can be changed into goodness is to set one's self above God; for He cannot do that. To do that would be to deny Himself, for He is righteousness.

God alone is good. This the Scriptures plainly declare. When Christ was on earth "there came one running, and kneeled to Him, and asked Him, Good Master, what shall I do that I may inherit eternal life? And Jesus said unto him, Why callest thou Me good? There is none good but one, that is God." Mark 10:17-18. Since God alone is good, it follows that for any one to claim that he has goodness in himself, is to make himself equal to God. The man who does that virtually makes himself God.

It is plain that if a man is to get righteousness he must get it from outside himself. He must, in fact, be made into another man. He must have a life entirely different from his natural life. This is dimly recognized in the frequently expressed desire to "live a different life." That is just what every one needs to do. The trouble is that so many try (fail) to live another life with the old life of sin, and that is impossible. In order for a man to live a different life from what he has been living it is necessary for him to have a different life.

From the text last quoted it is evident where he must get this life. God alone is good. His life is goodness itself. God's life consists of acts of goodness. One's life is just what his ways are, and all God's ways are right. The law of God expresses His ways, for we read, "Blessed are the undefiled in the way, who walk in the law of the Lord. Blessed are they that keep His testimonies, and that seek Him with the whole heart. They also do no iniquity: they walk in His ways." Psalms 119:1-3. And His ways are as much higher than man's ways as the heavens are higher than the earth.

Now the righteousness of God is a thing that man may have. The Saviour said to His disciples, "But seek ye first the kingdom of God, and His righteousness." Matthew 6.33. But where are we to seek for it? In Christ, because God has made Him unto us "wisdom, and righteousness, and sanctification, and redemption." 1 Corinthians 1.30. It is in Him that we may be made the righteousness of God. But since God's righteousness is His life, it is impossible for us to have His righteousness without having His life. This life is in Christ, for Christ is God, and God was in Christ, reconciling the world unto Himself. The only life ever lived on this earth that was perfectly righteous was the life of Christ. His life alone could resist sin. "Ye know that He was manifested to take away our sins; and in Him is no sin." 1 John 3:5. The life of Christ is the righteousness of God. It is that which we are to seek.

But man cannot live God's life. Only God can live His own life. It would be the height of presumption for any one to think that he could live the life of God. The life of God must be manifested in the man, if he has any righteousness, but God Himself must live the life. The

Apostle Paul expresses it thus: "I am crucified with Christ: nevertheless I live; yet not I, but Christ liveth in me: and the life which I now live in the flesh I live by the faith of the Son of God, who loved me, and gave Himself for me." Galatians 2:20.

Note again how easy it is for a man to set himself up as above God. Since righteousness is life, even the life of God, it is evident that for a man to claim that he has life in himself, - that he has by nature in himself a principle that cannot by any possibility die, - is the same as saying that he has righteousness in himself, and thus again to claim indirectly that he is God. This again is that man of sin.

It was this feeling that kept the Pharisees from accepting Christ. They "trusted in themselves that they were righteous." Luke 18:9. They professed to believe in eternal life, and searched the Scriptures with that in view; but Jesus sadly said to them, "Ye will not come to Me, that ye might have life." John 5:40. Why would they not come to Him, that they might have life? For the reason that they thought they had it in themselves. For righteousness is life. Christ came to this earth for the sole purpose of giving life to men, for they had forfeited life by sin. He gives His life to us, and that gives us His righteousness. The only reason why any one will not come to Christ for life is that he thinks that he has it already. Again we repeat, that whoever claims that one may have eternal life without Christ, thereby claims that one may have righteousness without Christ. The two must go together.

Let us read a few familiar texts, to impress this fact the more strongly on our minds. "For God so loved the world, that He gave His only begotten Son, that whosoever believeth in Him should not perish, but have everlasting life." John 3:16. "Thou hast given Him power over all flesh, that He should give eternal life to as many as thou hast given Him. And this is life eternal, that they might know Thee the only true God, and Jesus Christ, whom Thou has sent." John 17:2-3. "Verily, verily, I say unto you, "Except ye eat the flesh of the Son of man, and drink His blood, ye have no life in you." John 6:53. "As the living Father hath sent Me, and I live by the Father: so he that eateth Me, even he shall live by Me." John 6:57. This life in the man is the only way of righteousness. We are to be "made the righteousness of God in Him." 2 Corinthians 5:21.

This life is ours by faith, for the just shall live by faith. That does not mean that the life is not real, but that it can be retained only by faith. As the life is received, so must it be retained. "As ye have therefore received Christ Jesus the Lord, so walk ye in Him." Colossians 2:6. Man does not have this life in his own right, and within his own power. It is the life of God, and not the life of man. "This is the record, that God hath given to us eternal life, and this life is in His Son. He that hath the Son hath life; and he that hath not the Son of God hath not life." 1 John 5:11-12. It is the life of Jesus manifest in mortal flesh. 2 Corinthians 4:11.

This life is the light of men. "Then spake Jesus again unto them, saying, "I am the Light of the world: he that followeth Me shall not walk in darkness, but shall have the light of life." John 8:12. This life of righteousness is given to men as freely as the light of day. It is as abundant as the light; there is enough for all. A characteristic of light is that it can multiply itself. A single torch may light a thousand other torches, and still have as much light as in the beginning. So it is with the light of Christ's life. With Him is the fountain of life. It comes from Him in abundance. He can give life to every man in the world, if they would all receive it, and still have as much left as in the beginning. He can live in His fullness in every man. Every one who believes gets the benefit of the entire life of Christ. Christ is not divided.

Those who sit in the shadow of death, which is the shadow that sin casts, may have that shadow dispelled by allowing the light to shine in. That light is to be manifested in its fullness in the Church before the end, so that the life of Christ will be manifested before the world as plainly as when Christ was here on the earth in person. This will be the standard around which thousands will rally, even as they did on the day of Pentecost. It is this light of Christ's life of which the prophet speaks in these words: -

"Arise, shine, for thy light is come, and the glory of the Lord is risen upon thee. For, behold, the darkness shall cover the earth, and gross darkness the people: but the Lord shall arise upon thee, and His glory shall be seen upon thee. And the Gentiles shall come to thy light, and kings to the brightness of thy rising." Isaiah 60:1-3. All this, and much more is taught us in the simple words, "And God said, "Let there be light": and there was light."

Chapter 2—The Second Day

The clouds are the dust of his feet

"And God said, "Let there be a firmament in the midst of the waters, and let it divide the waters from the waters". And God made the firmament, and divided the waters from the waters. And God made the firmament, and divided the water, which were under the firmament from the waters, which were above the firmament: and it was so. And God called the firmament Heaven." Genesis 1:6-8.

On first thought it seems as though the work of the second day was very meager; but man's first thoughts of God's work are always very limited. Wonderful lessons of hope and comfort are to be learned from this day and are often referred to in the Bible as an example of the mighty power of God, and it will be remembered that the power of God is the hope of man. The Book of Job contains some magnificent descriptions of the power and majesty of God.

"He stretches out the north over the empty place, and hangeth the earth upon nothing. He bindeth up the waters in His thick clouds; and the cloud is not rent under them." Job 26:7-8. Who can ever tire of watching the clouds in their varying forms? They are a constant source of wonder. And then to think of the wonderful power that is represented by them! Think of the immense quantities of water that they hold, to pour out in the earth at the appointed time! It is the direct personal power of the Lord that causes it to rain. Science may tell us, in part, what conditions must obtain before rain falls, and may predict its occurrence with considerable accuracy; but this does not disprove the fact that God Himself orders the rain.

There are many things that man has observed in regard to the working of God, and there are many more that might be observed. That is what God wants us to do. "He has made His wonderful works to be remembered." Psalms 111.4. But He wants us to observe them only for the purpose of seeing Him in them. They who observe the works of God, only to attribute them to a goddess called Nature, as though God Himself were not concerned in them, study to no profit whatever. What men call Nature is simply that which is observed of the ways of God. No better definition has ever been given than this, that "the laws of nature are the habits of God." But after man has exhausted all his skill in observation and calculation concerning the ways of God, still he must remember that "these are but the outskirts of His ways: and how small a whisper do we hear of Him? But the thunder of his power who can understand?" Job 26:14. It is not possible for finite man to fathom all the ways of the infinite God, and therefore human science at its best is very limited.

We have said that it is the direct, personal power of the Lord that causes the rain. Read the following: "But the Lord is the true God; He is the living God, and an everlasting King: at His wrath the earth trembles, and the nations are not able to abide His indignation. Thus shall ye say unto them, The gods that have not made the heavens and the earth, these shall perish from the earth, and from under the heavens. He hath made the earth by His power, He hath established the world by His wisdom, and by his understanding hath He stretched out the heavens: when he uttereth His voice, there is a tumult of water i the heavens, and he causeth the vapors to ascend from the ends of the earth; He maketh lightnings for the rain, and bringeth forth the wind out of Hid treasuries." Jeremiah 10:10-13.

This is always designed to teach us the power of the word of God. Not only the simple power of the word of the Lord, but the wisdom of God, and the power by which He breathes upon us that word of righteousness. Read again from the book of Job. The twenty eighth chapter is one of the most perfect and sublime compositions ever known in any language, and from the latter part we quote these words: -

"Whence then cometh wisdom? And where is the place of understanding? Seeing it is hid from the eyes of all living, and kept close from the fowls of the air. Destruction and death say, "We have heard the fame thereof with our ears". God understandeth the way thereof, and He knoweth the place thereof.

For He looketh to the ends of the earth, and seeth under the whole heaven; to make the weight for the winds; and He weigheth the water by measure. When He made a decree for the rain, and a way for the lightning of the thunder: then did He see it, and declare it; He prepared it, yea, and searched it out. And unto man He said, Behold, the fear of the Lord, that is wisdom; and to depart from evil is understanding." Job 28:20-28.

The Psalmist tells us "the earth is full of the goodness of the lord." Psalms 33:5. From everything in nature God designs that we shall learn a lesson concerning Him and His love. God's servants in every age have learned some of these lessons. Especially did those holy men who were moved by the Spirit of God to utter His words see God in His works. But in these days, even as it was among the philosophers of old, men in their own fancied wisdom have not liked to retain God in their knowledge, and so have left Him out of their calculations. Too many, as they study the things of the earth and the heavens, instead of being filled with wonder and praise at the mighty power of God that is therein displayed, become filled with wonder at their own marvelous attainments, until they almost fancy that they have created the things that they have discovered. Men forget that these things existed ages before they were born, and almost imagine that their discovery of them is the bringing of them into existence. They speak with contemptuous pity of the men who wrote the Bible, as men who lived in an age inferior to ours, when "science" had not made any discoveries, and who were simple enough to think that these things which we see, and so readily account for, were the direct workings of God. Well, it is far better to be simple than to have so much wisdom that does not come from God, nor lead to Him.

But let us read the words of one, who was no mean scientist, the words of one whose wisdom was the wonder of his day in the whole world. A man to whom God Himself said, "Lo, I have given thee a wise and an understanding heart; so that there was none like thee before thee, neither after thee shall any arise like unto thee." I Kings 3:12. A man of whom the inspired word of God says, "He was wiser than all men; and his fame was in all nations round about. And he spake three thousand proverbs: and his songs were a thousand and five. And he spake of threes, from the cedar tree that is in Lebanon even unto the hyssop that springeth out of the wall: he spake also of beasts, and of fowl, and of creeping things, and of fishes. And there came of all people to hear the Wisdom of Solomon, from all kings of the earth, which had heard of his wisdom." I Kings 4:31-34.

In His proverbs he speaks much of the wonderful works of God, and in one of them he refers directly to the work that was done on the second day of creation week, and connects it with the word of God by which it was accomplished. Thus, "Who hath ascended up into heaven or descended? Who hath fathered the wind in his fists? Who hath bound the waters in garment? Who hath established all the ends of the earth? What is His name, and what is His Son's name, if thou canst tell? Every word of God is pure: He is a shield unto them that put their trust in him. Add thou not unto His word, lest He reprove thee, and thou be found a liar." Proverbs 30:4-6.

The rain which God has bound up in His thick clouds, and which His voice - the same voice that speaks peace and righteousness - causes to fall upon the earth, is a pledge to us of God's willingness to forgive. Listen to the holy boldness of the prophet Jeremiah: "We acknowledge, O Lord, our wickedness, and the iniquity of our fathers: for we have sinned against Thee. Do not abhor us, for Thy name's sake, do not disgrace the throne of Thy glory: remember; break not thy covenant with us. Are there any among the vanities of the Gentiles that can cause rain? Or can the heavens give showers? Art not Thou He, O Lord our God? Therefore we will wait upon Thee: for Thou hast made all these things." Jeremiah 14:20-22. The Lord is the One who causes rain; therefore we will wait upon Him, in confidence that

He will not abhor us, even though we have grievously sinned; but that He will, for the sake of His own word, pardon our iniquity.

Clouds And Showers Of Grace

Just as many people are frightened when they see clouds in the sky, so many people are needlessly troubled concerning clouds that arise before their minds. How often have we heard people say that they have known the blessing of the Lord, and have rejoiced in it, but that clouds have arisen of late, and they have no peace! Well, there are different ways of considering the clouds.

We may say that clouds are very unsubstantial things. The sun can dissipate them; and since the sun of Righteousness is ever shining, we need not go on under clouds of doubt. There is such a thing as getting above the clouds, and those who have had that experience can testify that it is a most glorious place to be in. Never have I been able to imagine a scene of more wonderful glory than burst upon my view one evening after I had long been toiling up the eastern slope of a mountain. We gained the top just before the sun set, and the valley on the other side was filled with clouds, lighted up by the splendor of the setting sun. It was not only a glorious sight for the eyes, but it impressed a lesson that can never be forgotten.

But more still should we remember when the clouds arise. God dwells in the midst of them. "The Lord reigneth; let the earth rejoice; let the multitude of isles be glad thereof. Clouds and darkness are round about Him: righteousness and judgment are the habitation of his throne." Psalms 97:1-2. It was from the midst of the cloud that God's law was given in love; and we know that "his commandment is life everlasting." John 12:50. Yea, even though the clouds are thick and dark, we will yet be glad, for God is there still. "He made darkness His secret place; His pavilion round about Him were dark waters and thick clouds of the skies." Psalms 18:1. The cloud that shuts out God from our sight is but the assurance to us of His presence.

From the clouds come rain, and this is a symbol of the free and abundant grace of God. When God calls us to buy of him wine and milk, without money and without price, - to come and find abundance of pardon, - He gives us this assurance: "For as the rain cometh down, and the snow from heaven, and returneth not thither, but watereth the earth, and maketh it bring forth and bud, that it may give seed to the sower, and bread to the eater: so shall My word not return unto Me void, but it shall accomplish that which I please, and it shall prosper in the thing whereto I sent it." Isaiah 55:10

As the water bound up in the thick clouds is to remind us of the mighty power of God, so it is to remind us of His Gospel of grace; for that is but the power of God unto salvation. The Gospel is the good news of salvation from sin, and everything that speaks the power of God tells us of the power He has to give us righteousness. "Drop down, ye heavens, from above, and let the skies pour down righteousness: let the earth open, and let them bring forth salvation, and let righteousness spring up together; I the Lord have created it." Isaiah 45:8. And carrying out the same figure, the prophet Hosea says: "Sow to yourselves in righteousness, reap in mercy: break up your fallow ground: for it is time to seek the Lord till He come and rain righteousness upon you." Hosea 10:12.

Thus from the power that is exhibited in the clouds that given rain upon the earth may we learn the power of that grace that will visit those who accept it, and will bring "showers of blessing."

"O worship the King, all glorious above,

And gratefully sing His wonderful love;

Our Shield and Defender, the Ancient of days,

Pavilioned in splendor, and girded with praise.

"O tell of His might, and sing of His grace.

Whose robe is the light; whose canopy, space;

His chariots of wrath the deep thunderclouds form,

And dark is His path on the wings of the storm.

"Thy bountiful care, what tongue can recite?

It breathes in the air; it shines in the light,

It streams from the hills; it descends to the plain,

And sweetly distils in the dew and the rain.

"Frail children of dust, and feeble as frail,

In Thee do we trust, nor find Thee to fail;

Thy mercies how tender! How firm to the end!

Our Maker, Defender, Redeemer, and Friend!"

The Bow Of Promise

There is a closer connection between the rain and the forgiveness of sins than many realize. When God made a covenant with Noah, that He could no more destroy the world by a flood, He said: "This is the token of the covenant which I make between Me and you and every living creature that is with you, for perpetual generations: I do set My bow in the cloud, and it shall be for a token of a covenant between Me and the earth. And it shall come to pass, when I bring a cloud over the earth, that the bow shall be seen in the cloud: and I will remember My covenant, which is between Me and you and every living creature of all flesh; and the waters shall no more become a flood to destroy all flesh. And the bow shall be in the cloud; and I will look upon it, that I may remember the everlasting covenant between God and every living creature of all flesh that is upon the earth," Genesis 9:12-16.

God said, "I do set My bow in the cloud." The rainbow is in a special sense God's bow, for it is that which encircles His throne. When John, on the Isle of Patmos, saw the throne of God in heaven, he saw that "there was a rainbow round about the throne, insight like unto an emerald." Revelation 4.3. The prophet Ezekiel also saw "visions of God," He saw "the likeness of a throne, as the appearance of a sapphire stone: and upon the likeness of the throne was the likeness as the appearance of a man above upon it. And I saw as the color of amber, as the appearance of fire round about within it, from the appearance of his loins even upward, and from the appearance of his loins even downward, I saw as it were the appearance of fire, and it had brightness round about. As the appearance of the bow that is in the cloud in the day of rain, so was the appearance of the brightness round about. This was the appearance of the likeness of the glory of the Lord." Ezekiel 1:26-28.

We learn, therefore, that when God sets his bow in the clouds, He puts there His own glory that is about His throne. It is the bow of promise, for He gave His word, and His word is His glory. Thus it was that Jeremiah, on pleading for forgiveness for the people of God, said, "do not disgrace the throne of Thy glory." Jeremiah 14.21. For God to break his word would be to make His glorious bow of no effect; and as that is some of the glory of his throne, it would be to disgrace the throne of His glory.

We learn from the prophecy that the bow in the cloud, which is the token of the steadfastness of God's word, not only assures us that there will be no more flood, but that it is an assurance of the mercy of God in the forgiveness of sins. To His people God says: "For a small moment have I forsaken thee; but with great mercies will I gather thee. In a little wrath I hid My face from thee for a moment; but with everlasting kindness will I have mercy on thee, saith the Lord thy Redeemer. For this is as the waters of Noah should no more go over the earth; so have I sworn that i would not be wroth with thee, nor rebuke thee. For the mountains shall depart, and the hills be removed; but my kindness shall not depart from thee, neither shall the covenant of My peace be removed, saith the Lord that hath mercy on thee." Isaiah 54:7-10.

Let the cloud of sins be never so thick and threatening, the glory of God's word of grace shining upon it will bring into full view the bow of promise, and we shall remember that there is forgiveness with Him, that He may be feared. So even the clouds of darkness that overshadow the earth may bear to us a message of comfort.

"Ye fearful saints, fresh courage take; the clouds ye so much dread

Are big with mercy, and shall break in blessings o'er your head."

Chapter 3—The Third Day

The fullness of the sea

"And God said, "Let the waters under the heaven be gathered together unto one place, and let the dry land appear": and it was so. And God called the dry land Earth; and the gathering together of the water called He Seas; and God saw that it was good." Genesis 1:9-10. When, as recorded in the last part of the Book of Job, the Lord would convince the patriarch of his weakness and dependence upon God, that he might know that righteousness comes from God alone, He referred to this gathering together of the waters as proof. "Who shut up the sea with doors, when it brake forth, as if it had issued out of the womb? When I made the cloud the garment thereof, and thick darkness a swaddling band for it, and prescribed for it My decree, and set bars and doors, and said, Hitherto shalt thou come, but no further: and here shall thy proud waves be stayed." Job 38:8-11

When the Psalmist speaks of the power of the word, by which God created the heavens and the earth, he says, "He gathereth the waters of the sea together as an heap: He layeth up the depth in storehouses." Psalms 33.7 It may be well to notice here, in passing, the words, "And it was so," with which the record of every new step in creation is closed. God said, "Let it be," - "and it was so." His simple word was sufficient to establish it. Let it be remembered that this is the word, which by the Gospel is preached unto us. Its power has never diminished; it is as able to save, as it was to create.

It is impossible that any one who is acquainted to any degree with the Lord should stand by the sea without being reminded of the mighty power of the Creator. Yet many gaze upon the sea day after day with never a thought of its Maker, and even openly defy Him. To such the Lord says: "Hear now this, O foolish people, and without understanding: which have eyes, and see not; which have ears, and hear not:

"Fear ye not Me? Saith the Lord: will ye not tremble at My presence, which have placed the sand for the bound of the sea by a perpetual decree, that it cannot pass it: and though the waves thereof toss themselves, yet can they not prevail; though they roar, yet can they not pass over it?" Jeremiah 5:21-22.

But it is not in order to produce fright that the Lord reminds us of His mighty power that can set bounds for the sea, so that it cannot pass over in its fiercest tumult. No; it is that we may trust Him. Perfect faith and love drive fear away. So the power of God over the sea is referred to as evidence of His faithfulness. "O Lord God of hosts, who is a strong Lord like unto Thee? Or to Thy faithfulness round about Thee? Thou rules the raging of the sea: When the waves thereof arise, Thou stillest them." Psalms 89.8,9. An example of this faithfulness is given in the Gospels. "And the same day, when the even was come, He saith unto them, Let us pass over unto the other side. And when they had sent away the multitude, they took Him even as He was in the ship. And there were also with Him other little ships. And there arose a great storm of wind, and the waves beat into the ship, so that it was now full. And He was in the hinder part of the ship, asleep on a pillow: and they awake Him, and say unto him, Master, carest Thou not that we perish? And He arose, and rebuked the wind, and said unto the sea, Peace, be still. And the wind ceased, and there was a great calm. And He said unto them, Why are ye so fearful? How is it that ye have no faith? And they feared exceedingly, and said one to another, 'What manner of Man is this, that even the wind and the sea obey Him?'" Mark 4:35-41.

This was but the manifestation of the original creative power. He who created the heavens and the earth, the sea, and all that in them is, retains full control over all. In those words, "Peace, be still," we hear the came voice that said, "Let the waters under the heaven be gathered together into one place." And this is the word which by the Gospel is preached to us; so we are to learn from God's power over the sea, which is His because He made it, His power over the waves of strife that surge through human hearts.

For the angry sea represents the wicked. "The wicked are like the troubled sea, when it cannot rest, whose waters cast up mire and dirt." Isaiah 57:20. Christ is our peace. The word which He spoke to the sea of Galilee that night is the word which He speaks to us. "I will hear what God the Lord will speak: For He will speak peace unto His people, and to His saints: but let them not turn again to folly." Psalms 85:8. Surely here is comfort for those who have long struggled in vain with fierce passions.

Not only is God's power over the sea a symbol of His power to save men from the tide of sin, but it is also a pledge and surety of their final complete deliverance. It also shows the power with which God is going to clothe the preaching of the Gospel message in the last struggle preceding His second coming. Read the following soul-thrilling words: -

"Awake, awake, put on strength, O arm of the Lord; awake, as in the days of old, the generations of ancient times. Art thou not it that cut Rahab [Egypt] in pieces that pierced the dragon? Art thou not it which dried up the sea, the waters of the great deep; that made the depths of the sea a way for the redeemed to pass over? And the ransomed of the Lord shall return, and come with singing unto Zion: and everlasting joy shall be upon their heads: they shall obtain gladness and joy, and sorrow and sighing shall flee away. I, even I, am He that comforteth you: who art thou, that thou art afraid of man that shall die, and of the son of man which shall be made as grass; and hast forgotten the Lord thy Maker, that stretched forth the heavens, and laid the foundation of the earth; and fearest continually all the day because of the fury of the oppressor? The captive exile shall speedily be loosed; and he shall not die and go down into the pit, neither shall his bread fail. For I am the Lord thy God, which stirreth up the sea that the waves thereof roar: the lord of hosts is His name. And I have put My word in thy mouth, and have covered thee in the shadow of Mine hand, the I may plant the heavens, and lay the foundations of the earth, and say unto Zion, Thou art My People." Isaiah 51:9-16.

Surely the fact that "the sea is His and He made it,"1 and that He "Hath measured the waters in the hollow of His hand," (Isaiah 40.12) is sufficient ground for confidence in him by any of His people, whether it be for deliverance from danger, for overcoming grace, or for help in carrying on the work to which He has called them.

"Christ In The Tempest"

"Storm on the midnight waters. The vast sky

Is stooping with the thunder. Cloud on cloud

Reels heavily in the darkness, like a shroud

Shook by some warning spirit from the high

And terrible wall of heaven. The mighty wave

Tosses beneath its shadow, like the bold

Upheavings of a giant from the grave

Which bound him prematurely to its cold

And desolate bosom. Lo, they mingle now-

Tempest and heaving wave, along whose brow

Trembles the lightning from its thick fold.

"And it is very terrible. The roar

Ascendeth into heaven, and thunders break

Like a response of demons from the black
Rifts of the hanging tempest - yawning o'er
The wild waves in their torment. Hark! the cry
Of the strong man in peril, piercing through
The uproar of the waters and the sky;
As the rent bark one moment rides to view
On the tall billows, with the thunder-cloud
Closing around above her like a shroud.
"He stood upon the reeling deck. His form
Made visible by the lightning, and His brow
Uncovered to the visiting of the storm,
Told of a triumph man may never know-
Power underived and mighty. 'Peace, be still.'
The great waves heard Him, and the storm's loud tones
Went moaning into silence at His will;
And the thick clouds, where yet the lightning shone,
And slept the latent thunder, roller away
Until no trace of tempest lurked behind,
Changing upon the pinions of the wind
To stormless wanderers, beautiful and gay.
"Dread Ruler of the tempest! Thou before
Whose presence boweth the uprisen storm;
To whom the waves do homage round the shore
Of many an island empire! If the form
Of the frail dust beneath Thine eye may claim
Thine infinite regard, O breathe upon
The storm and darkness of man's soul the same

> *Quiet and peace and humbleness which came*
> *O'er the roused water where thy voice had gone,*
> *A minister of peace - to conquer in Thy name."*
> Early poem by J.G. Whittier

A Lesson From The Grass

"And God said, Let the earth bring forth grass, the herb yielding seed, and the fruit tree yielding fruit after his kind, whose seed is in itself, upon the earth: and it was so. And the earth brought forth grass, and herb yielding seed after his kind, and the tree yielding fruit, whose seed was in itself, after his kind: and God saw that it was good." Genesis 1:11-12.

God said, "Let it be so," and it was so. "He spake and it was: He commanded, and it stood fast." And that word liveth and abideth forever. It never loses any of its life and force. The lapse of time does not diminish its power. The word, which created all things, upholds all things. Consequently that command, "Let the earth bring forth grass," is still causing the earth to bring forth grass, and herbs, and trees. If the effect of that word had ceased as soon as it was spoken, then there never would have been any more grass. The grass that was brought forth would have ceased to exist. And especially after the fall of man had brought the curse upon the earth, and death had come not only to man, but to animals and plants, if the word by which the grass was brought forth in the beginning had not been in full force, the earth would speedily have become a barren waste. But that word still lives, and therefore we have the earth clothed with grass, and abundance of fruit for the food of man.

This is not a mere theory, but it is a practical fact. That which is so common a thing, as the growth of grass, ceases to call forth our wonder, and we get to thinking that it simply grows of itself, without any interposition on the part of God. Indeed, most people would think that it is beneath the dignity of God to pay any attention to so small a thing as the growing of grass. That is just the reason why so few people derive any practical benefit from their professed faith in God. Their idea of God is of some being far off, who has so much to do with attending to His own affairs of State that He has no time to look after the details of His kingdom. They forget that looking after and caring for His creatures, from the greatest to the smallest, is the especial work of God. They forget that His greatness consists in His ability to manage the most stupendous affairs, and at the same time to pay attention to the smallest details.

Satan is well pleased to have men regard God as One who does not trouble Himself with their small affairs. That is just the charge, which he brings against God, and it is only at his suggestion that men have adopted it. Leaving aside the matter of evolution in its most extreme phase, considered for a minute the very common idea that in the beginning God did indeed set the universe in motion; but that He then endowed matter with a certain amount of force, and subjected it to certain definite laws, so that everything should run for ever after much the same as a clock that has been wound up and left to itself. With what confidence can one who holds such a view offer prayer? What can he expect to receive? No wonder that people complain that their prayers are not answered. The god that they worship is too far off to hear their prayers, and too indifferent, or too rigidly circumscribed by the laws which He has laid down, to interfere in their behalf if He has laid down, to interfere in their behalf if He should hear. Such a God is not the God of the Bible.

It is not a trivial matter that "the latest deductions of science" have drawn so many professed believers in the Bible to modify their views of the story of creation. The time was when men believed that the Bible means what it says. The men in whom God wrought mightily to the conversion of thousands were men of faith, and their faith was in the Divine power that made the heavens and the earth, and in the word, which upholds even the smallest of things. Their belief and practical application of the fact that God lives, and that everything is within His power, and under His immediate control, was what sustained them to battle with difficulties and dangers; it was the source of their strength, and the secret of their success.

But now what a change has taken place! It is a very rare thing to find a minister of the Gospel who dares risk his reputation enough to express a belief in the literalness of the story of creation in the first chapter of Genesis. They are afraid that they will be thought "behind the times." Would to God that there were more men willing to be behind these perilous times, and not afraid to be counted fools for Christ's sake.

As men have become afraid to believe the word of the Lord, lest they should disagree with that philosophy which is only a legacy handed down from ancient heathenism, the power of the word has not been openly manifested. It has been given too little opportunity. Christians pray for a revival of religion. If they would but revive belief in the simple word of God, and recognize it as al living thing, and as the source of all life and power, there would be a revival of religion. Let the Gospel be preached, not with wisdom of men, but in the words which the Holy Ghost teacheth; let it be set forth as the living, active word of God, and men will believe, and it will be seen to work effectually in those that believe. (1 Thessalonians 2:13).

There could be no more sure way to undermine the Gospel, and rob it of its power, than the substitution of the teachings of "Science falsely so called "for the simple word of God. God has been relegated to the rear, and is regarded as afar off. So, although many did accept that Gospel which is preached to them, and do sincerely wish salvation from sin, evolution, even though they have no conscious belief in it, has so taken the edge off of faith that they are not able to come close to the Lord, to walk and talk with Him, and to make Him an active Factor in every affair of life.

But let us note some simple facts that will justify one, even in this scientific age, in believing that the word of the Lord, which in the beginning said, "Let the earth bring forth grass," is still causing the earth to bring forth grass. Who has not watched the springing forth of the tender blade of grass or corn? Have you not at times passed along by the field of corn, and noticed a tiny blade pushing its way to the surface, in spite of heavy clods of earth? Have you not seen a portion of the baked earth heaved up, and, looking beneath, have seen that a tiny spire held it up, so tender that it could not support its own weight if released from its position? The blade had as yet scarcely any color, and was but little more than water, for if you had crushed it in your fingers there would have been scarcely anything but moisture on your hand. Yet this tiny thing was pushing away from before it a clod of earth ten thousand times its own weight.

Whence comes this power? Is it something that is inherent in the grass? Try it, and see. Take that blade of grass that is full grown. Select a small clod of earth, not half the size of the one that was pushed away from be fore it when it was crowding its way to the surface of the ground, and put it upon the grass. What is the result? Anybody can tell you. The grass is crushed to the ground. It has no power in itself. Test it again. Take that blade that is pushing its way to the surface from beneath that clod, and remove it from the ground. You take it in you fingers, and it lops down over the side of your hand. It cannot stand upright. Scarcely anything can be thought of that is weaker, and yet but a few moment before it was standing erect, and bearing a burden infinitely heavier than itself. Here is a miracle that is wrought hundreds of millions of times every year, and yet there are those who say that the age of miracles is past.

Will any scientist tell what is the source of the marvelous power exhibited in the grass, or in the bursting of the hard shell of the peach stone by the little germ within? There is something there that no microscope can discover, and no chemical analysis can detect. We can see the manifestation of Power, but cannot see the power it self. Skeptics may sneer if they please, but we are content to believe that the power is nothing else than the power of God's word. The word of the Lord said in the beginning, "Let the earth bring forth grass," and the power of that word causes the grass to spring forth in spite of all the clods of earth. There is no power in the grass, but that most feeble instrument is used to exhibit to man the mighty power of God. In that every man may learn a lesson - if he will.

Did I say that we were content to believe that it is the power of the word of God that is manifested in the blade of grass? Nay, not content merely, but glad that we can recognize God's power in small things. In that we see the assurance that God is able to do for us "exceeding abundantly above all that we ask or think, according to the power that worketh in us." Ephesians 3:20. For the same power that worked in the grass of the field also worked in the man who puts his trust in the lord. "All flesh is grass." Isaiah 40:6. Man is as weak and frail as the grass, having absolutely no power in himself; yet he is able to do all things through Christ, who strengthens him. Recall again the "voice pictures." There we saw that the voice of man can produce the forms of living things; but the voice of God produces the very living things themselves.

Not only do the grass, the trees, and the myriad forms of fruits and flowers grow in obedience to the command of the Lord, but they are the visible representation of His voice. In nature we see the voice of God, and that is the basis of our trust in that word when we read it in the Scriptures. It was not an accident that the eleventh chapter of Hebrews, which is a record of some of the mighty works that have been wrought in feeble men by simple faith in the word of God, begins with the statement that "by faith we understand that the worlds were framed by the word of God." Men may smile at the simplicity of

> "The poor Indian, whose untutored mind
>
> Sees God in clouds, and Hears Him in the wind,"

But better far that "untutored mind" than the mind filled with the "instruction that causes to err from the words of knowledge." Proverbs 19.27

To us Christ says, as well as to His disciples of old, "Ye have not chosen Me, but I have chosen you, and ordained you, that ye should go and bring forth fruit, and that your fruit should remain." John 15:16. We to bring forth fruit by the same power that causes the natural fruit of the earth to grow. That word which said, "Let the earth bring for the grass, and herb yielding seed after his kind, and the tree yielding fruit," and whose power we can see manifested in the grass and trees, says to us, "Bring forth fruit"; and if we are willing to be as submissive to the word as is the inanimate creation, the fruit will be as abundant. But take notice that the fruit is to be to the glory of God. "Herein is My Father glorified, the ye bear much fruit." John 15:8. If the power to bear the fruit were in us, there would be nothing to the glory of God; but what ever fruit is borne is to the glory of god; but whatever fruit is borne is to the glory of God, because the power is all from Him. We, like the grass, are but the powerless instrument through which God manifests His own power.

The Divine command is, "Grow in grace, and in the knowledge of our Lord and Saviour Jesus Christ." 2 Peter 3:18. We also grow just as the seed grows in the ground. Hear the words of Christ: "So is the kingdom of God, as if a man should cast seed upon the earth; and should sleep and rise night and day, and the seed should spring up and grow, he knoweth not how." Mark 4:26-27. We may not know how the good seed of the word of God springs up within us, to cause to bring forth fruit, but that makes no difference. "God giveth it a body as it hath pleased Him." Our part is to yield to the Divine Husband man; His part is to cause the growth and the perfect fruit.

The growth of plants is again and again use in the Scriptures as illustrating Christian growth. The Apostle Paul says: "Ye are God's husbandry" (1 Corinthians 3:9), or tilled land. So the Lord says, "The Spirit of the Lord God is upon Me; because the lord hath anointed Me to preach good tidings unto the meek; He hath sent Me to bind up the brokenhearted, to proclaim liberty to them that are bound; to appoint unto them that mourn in Zion, to give unto them beauty for ashes, the oil of joy for mourning, the garment of praise for the spirit of heaviness; that they might be call ed trees of righteousness, the planting of the Lord, that He might be glorified." Isaiah 41:1-3.

Bear in mind that the whole thing is of the Lord. We are His tillage. We are His planting, that He might be glorified. But note further how likeness to the growth of plants is carried out. See how salvation from sin, -a life of righteousness, -is indeed as when one casts seed upon the earth.

"I will greatly rejoice in the Lord, my soul shall be joy in My God; for He hath clothed Me with the garments of salvation, He hath covered Me with the robe of righteousness, as a bridegroom decks himself with ornaments, and as a bride adorns herself with her jewels. For as the earth bringeth forth her bud, and as the garden causeth the things that are sown in it to spring forth; so the Lord God will cause righteousness and praise to spring forth before all the nations." Isaiah 61:10-11.

It is wonderful what God can do if we will only let Him. Does some one say, "If He is so powerful, why does He not have His way in spite of us?" Because His power is the power of Love, and Love does not use force. God wants everybody in the universe to be satisfied, and so He gives to all the right of perfect freedom of choice as to what they will have. He tells them the relative value of things, and begs of them to choose that which is good; but if any are determined to have that which is evil, He lets them have it. He will have free men in His kingdom, and not a race of slaves and prisoners. Such they would be, if He compelled them to have salvation against their will. He wants subjects whom He can trust in any part of the universe; but if He were to compel any to be saved, He would still have to exercise force to retain them in the kingdom. Christ came to preach deliverance to the captives, and He does not propose to deliver them to bondage.

But when any one wants salvation, no matter how small and weak he is, no matter how insignificant he may be in the eyes of the world, even thought he be regarded no more than the grass which is trodden under foot, God can work wonders with him. If God so clothes the grass of the fields, which today is, and tomorrow is cast into the oven, much more will He clothe with power the men whom He has made in His own image, if they but submit to Him. That promise that He will clothe us does not refer exclusively to clothing for the body. "The life is more than meat, and the body than raiment." Matthew 6:25. He gives us that which is of infinite value. So the promise that He will much more clothe us than the grass refers as well to the garment of salvation and the robe of righteousness, with which we are to be clothed. That power which worked so wonderfully in the tiny blade of grass will work still more mightily in the man who trusts the Lord.

"Consider the lilies of the field, how they grow." Matthew 6:28. I have said that this is written for our encouragement in our growth in grace. As they grow, so must we. Now read some words of Inspiration, which show clearly that the growth of the lily is but an illustration of the Christian's growth in grace: -

"O Israel, return unto the Lord Thy God; for thou hast fallen by thine iniquity. Take with you words, and turn to the Lord: say unto Him, Take away all iniquity, and receive us graciously: so will we render the calves [offerings] of our lips. Asshur shall not save us; we will not ride upon horses: neither will we say any more to the work of our hands, 'Ye are our gods': for in Thee the fatherless findeth mercy." Hosea 14:1-3. There is no doubt but that it is sin and righteousness that the Lord is here speaking of. He tells His people, who have departed from Him, to return, and He tells them what to say when they return. Note that they are to say that they will not any more trust in the work of their hands. Their works are not to be from self, but those that are wrought in God. Now see the assurance that He gives those who thus turned away from him: -

"I will heal their backsliding, I will love them freely: for mine anger is turned away from him. I will be as the dew unto Israel: he shall grow as the lily, and cast forth his roots as Lebanon. His branches shall spread, and his beauty shall be as the olive tree, and his smell as Lebanon. They that dwell under his shadow shall return; they shall revive as the corn, and grow [margin, blossom] as the vine." Hosea 14:4-7.

But this is not all. God's people are His vineyard, the branch of His planting, that He might be glorified; and He would not be glorified if through any lack of personal attention they should be destroyed. So He assures them of His constant care. "In that day sing ye unto her, a vineyard of red wine. I the Lord do keep it; I will water it every moment: lest any hurt it, I will keep it night and day. Fury is not in Me: who would set the briers and thorns against Me in battle? I would go through them, I would burn them together. Or let him take hold of My strength, that he may make peace with Me; and he shall make peace with Me He shall cause them that come of Jacob to take root: Israel shall blossom and bud, and fill the face of the world with fruit." Isaiah 27:2-6

But what need of carrying the likeness any further? We could not exhaust the Scriptures if we should try. And the only design of this writing is to lead the reader to study the word more closely for himself, and to appropriate it as the living word of the living God, which works effectually in all that believe. Do not put the Lord off, but let you faith prove that He is near, even a very present Help in trouble. He is a God nigh at hand, and not afar off; and nothing is too hard for Him. He has written His love and His power upon all Creation, and wants to speak to us through the things that He has made. In Him all things consist. That same word that spoke the universe into existence, which said to the earth, "Bring forth grass," speaks to us in the words of God's law. But His law is not a hard, lifeless decree, which weak mortals are to strive in vain to keep, while God watches them with a stern eye, ready to taunt and punish them for failure; but we "know that His commandment is life everlasting." John 12:50. That word which says to us, "Thou shalt love the Lord thy God with all thy heart, and thy neighbor as thyself," sheds that love abroad in our hearts, just as the word of God brings forth the fruit in the plant. Then well may we sing: -

> "How gentle God's commands!
>
> How kind His precepts are!
>
> Come, cast your burdens on the Lord,
>
> And trust His constant care.
>
> "Beneath His watchful eye
>
> His saint securely dwell;
>
> That hand that bears all nature up
>
> Shall guard His children well.

"Why should this anxious load
Press down your weary mind?
Haste to your Heavenly Father's throne,
And sweet refreshment find.
"His goodness stands approved
Through each succeeding day;
I'll drop my burden at His feet,
And bear a song away."

Chapter 4—The Fourth Day

The firmament showeth his handiwork

In no part of the creation of God do we find more wonderful Gospel lessons than in the heavens. We have already seen that the heavenly bodies preach the Gospel, although they have no articulate speech. The Apostle Paul, having stated that all had not obeyed the Gospel, adds that faith cometh by hearing, and hearing by the word of God, and then asks, "But I say, 'Have they not heard?'" Heard what? Why, the Gospel, of course. And then he answers his own question, saying, "Yes, verily," and proves it by quoting the words of the Psalmist concerning the heavens, "Their sound went into all the earth, and their words unto the ends of the world." Romans 10:15-18. The heavens, therefore, do most widely and powerfully preach the Gospel. Let us note a few points from the word, that we may be able henceforth more readily to read the language of the heavens.

"The heavens declare the glory of God; and the firmament showeth His handiwork." Psalms 19:1. Now put with this a statement concerning man. "For we are His workmanship, created in Christ Jesus unto good works, which God hath before ordained [prepared] that we should walk in them." Ephesians 2:10. The same language is used about us that is used of the heavens. Both are His workmanship, and both are created in Christ, provided we yield ourselves to Him. That thing for which we are created is good works, by which we are to glorify our Father, which is in heaven. So if we have the good works, we, as well as the heavens, declare the glory of God.

The heavens do the work that God has appointed for them. They do it because they are perfectly subject to his will. So if we are as subject to Him, we shall do the work that He has appointed for us. And that work glorifies Him, because it is He that does the work in us. Notice that God has before prepared these works that we should walk in them. So Christ says of the one who does the truth, that he comes to the light, "that his deeds may be made manifest, that they are wrought in God." God Himself does the works; else they would not be the righteousness of God. That which the heavens do is also His work; and when we are voluntarily as submissive to His will as they are by nature, then the glory of God will be as fully declared by us as by them, even though, like them, were unable to make an articulate sound.

The heavens are the pledge of God's faithfulness. "I will sing of the mercies of the Lord for ever: with my mouth will I make known Thy faithfulness to all generations. For I have said, Mercy shall be built up for ever; Thy faithfulness shalt Thou establish in the very heavens." Psalms 89:1-2. The existence of the heavens is a surety that God has not forgotten His promises of mercy to men. The thirty-first chapter of the prophet Jeremiah is full of the "exceeding great and precious promise to His people, "I will forgive their iniquity, and I will remember their sin no more," there follows this: "Thus saith the Lord, which giveth the sun for a light by day, and the ordinances of the moon and of the stars for a light by night, which divideth the sea when the waves thereof roar; The Lord of hosts is His name; if those ordinances depart form before Me, saith the Lord, then the seed of Israel also shall cease from being a nation before me for ever." Jeremiah 31:34-36. So long as the sun, moon, and stars fulfill their appointed work regularly, the sons of me can find mercy with the Lord. So long may the come to Him, and find pardon, peace, and righteousness.

The Oath Of God

There is more to this. "For when God made promise to Abraham, because He could swear by no greater, He sware by Himself." this was an oath for the confirmation of the promise, which was in itself immutable. Moreover, the promise the immutability of His counsel, confirmed it by an oath: that by two immutable things, in which it was impossible for God to lie, we might have a strong consolation who have fled for refuge to lay hold upon the hope set before us: Which hope we have as an anchor of the soul, both sure and steadfast, which entereth into that within the veil; whither the forerunner is for us entered even Jesus, made an High Priest for ever after the order of Melchisedec." Hebrews 6:13, 17-20.

Mark two things: First, this oath and promise were given for our sakes. Abraham did not need that God should confirm the promise with an oath, for he had demonstrated to the full that he believed the Lord's simple word. But God gave the oath so that we might have our faith in His word strengthened. Second, the oath and the promise relate to the forgiveness of sins, and all the blessing, which Christ as our High Priest secures for us. They are for our consolation and encouragement when we flee for refuge too Christ. Therefore when we come to Christ for mercy, and grace to help in time of need, we are assured beforehand by the promise of God, backed up by His oath, that we shall have the things for which we ask. How let us stop and think for a moment what this means.

The oath of God is really a pledging of His own existence. He swore by Himself. He has thereby declared that His life would be forfeited if His promise should fail. His promises are as enduring as Himself. As God is "from everlasting to everlasting." so "the mercy of the Lord is from everlasting to everlasting upon them that fear Him." Psalms 103:17. The Father and the son are one. So in God's pledging Himself, Christ is pledged. But "in Him were all things created, in the heavens and upon the earth, things visible and things in visible, whether thrones or dominions or principalities or powers; all things have been created through Him, and unto Him: and He is before all things, and in Him all things consist." Colossians 1:16-17. It is "by the word of His power" that all things are upheld. Hebrews 1:3.

Upon the existence of God depends the existence of the heavens and the earth. But He has pledged His own existence to the fulfillment of His promises. Therefore the existence of the heavens, yea, of the entire universe, depends upon the fulfillment of the promises of God to the believing sinner. If a single sinner, no matter how unworthy, or insignificant, or obscure, should come to the Lord sincerely asking for pardon and holiness, and should fail to receive it, that instant the whole universe would become chaos, and vanish out of existence. But the sun, moon, and stars still hold their places in heavens, as a proof that God has never failed a single soul that put his trust in Him, and as a pledge that His mercies fail not. His faithfulness, therefore, is in the heavens. If we would let the sun, moon, and stars tell this story to us every time we see them, we should live better lives, and discouragement should be a thing unknown.

God Is A Sun And Shield

"For the Lord God is a sun and shield." Psalms 84:11. As the sun gives light and heat to the earth, so the Lord is the Light of men, and warms them by his grace. All the heat and light that the earth receives, in whatever form, comes from the sun. The light by means of which we find our way at night through the crowded streets of the city, or by which we read in our study, comes from the sun. So with the cheerful wood blaze, or the glowing coals that warm out rooms in dreary winter, all the heat comes from the sun.

The sun gives light, and light is life. How the plants turn to the sun! Who has not noticed a plant growing in a dark cellar? Its life is very feeble. In the darkness it is almost dead. But let an opening be made, so that a ray of light can shine through, and at once it revives. It will begin to grow in the direction of the light. Without light, which the sun furnishes to the earth, there should be no plant life, or animal life either.

But life means growth. As the light of the sun is the life of plants, so it is the cause of their growth. As the plant grows, it is by storing up the light and heat of the sun. Those plants that grow very quickly, that come to maturity from the seed in few weeks or months have in them but very little heat. They are worthless for fuel. But the sturdy oak, that is centuries in growing, -which grows so slowly that in a year no difference can be detected in its size, -

stores up immense quantities of the sun's heat. Other trees are of even slower growth, and store up more heat.

These woods become buried in the ground, and in the course of centuries are transformed into coal. Then it is used as fuel, and gives to us the heat, which it has stored up from the sun. The reason why we get so much more heat from the coal than from the direct rays of the sun is, that in the coal we have the concentrated heat of the sun's rays for years.

What the sun is to the earth, and to plant life, that God is to His people. "The Lord God is a sun." As the sun, by its light, gives physical life to the plants, so God gives spiritual life - the only real life - to His people. Christ's life is the light of the world. As the oak-tree stores up the heat of the sun, so the one who lives in the light of God stores up that light, which is His life. That light and life that are the life and growth of the Christian are to be given out for the enlightenment and warmth of others.

Some one may say, that in order to carry out the figure completely, it ought to be that the Christian of the slowest growth should have the most of the life of God to live out. But let it not be forgotten that the just live by faith. The Christian's life is not measured by years, but by the faith manifested. The more faith, which means humility and trust, the more of the life of God is appropriated. And the more life appropriated, the more will be given out to others, for the life of God cannot be hidden.

Grace and Glory

Again we quote, "For the Lord God is a sun and shield: the Lord will give grace and glory." Psalms 84:11. Of what use is it for the Lord to speak to us of glory? What do we know about it? Why, we have it before us every day. "The heavens declare the glory of God: and the firmament showeth His Handiwork." Psalms 19:1. Still more plainly does the Psalmist put it in these word, "O Lord our Lord, how excellent is Thy name in all the earth! Who hast set Thy glory above the heavens." Psalms 8:1. The heavens declare the glory. The glory of the sun when it shines in its strength is but the reflected glory of the Lord. That glory in which God dwells - the light which no man can approach unto - is partly revealed in the firmament. So it is true in the most literal sense, that Christ, the great Creator, is the light of the world.

But grace and glory are equal and interchangeable. Thus we read that Christ is the brightness of the Father's glory. The Revised Version has it, "the effulgence of His glory." "But unto every one of us is given grace according to the measure of the gift of Christ." Ephesians 4:7. He is "full of grace and truth," and "of His fullness have all we received, and grace for grace." John 1:14-16. Therefore it is evident that grace and glory are the same in measure. When God gives grace, it is according to the riches of His glory; and when He gives glory, it is according to the riches of His grace. This will appear still more plainly.

There is power in the glory of God. Christ was raised from the dead "by the glory of the Father." Romans 6:4. The inspired prayer for us is, that we may be "strengthened with all power, according to the might of His glory." Colossians 1:11. What this power is the heavens reveal. It is the power that holds them in their places. It is the power that they exert over the earth, the power by which all life is maintained. As we behold the glory of the sun, or of the heavens when they are studded with stars, and the moon is at her full, we may remember that they in their splendor are declaring the glory of God, and therefore are telling of the fullness and power of His grace, which is shed on us abundantly through Jesus Christ our Saviour.

God's glory is his goodness. The apostle tells us "all have sinned, and come short of the glory of God." Romans 3:23. Mark well that the coming short of the glory of God consists in the fact that men have sinned. If they had not sinned, they would not have come short of the glory of God. Therefore it is evident that the goodness of God is His glory. But it is the goodness of God that leads man to repentance. Romans 2:4. And the Psalmist says, "Oh how great is Thy goodness, which Thou hast laid up for them that fear Thee; which Thou hast wrought for them that trust in Thee before the sons of men!" Psalms 31:19. It is His goodness, or righteousness, which we are to seek, and which is put into and upon every one that believes. The goodness of God conceived the plan of redemption. But, "be grace are ye saved." Therefore the grace of God is simply the manifestation to men of His goodness, and His goodness is His glory; therefore the grace and the glory of God are in reality the same thing.

"The Lord will give grace and glory." When will He give these? Is it grace now and glory hereafter? No! He gives both now to those that take Him. He gives glory now in the form of grace, and grace hereafter in the form of glory. Hear the words of Christ, who is the brightness of the glory of God, when He prayed the Father, "Glorify Thou Me with Thine own self with the glory which I had with Thee before the world was." Speaking of His disciples (not merely the twelve, but all who should believe on Him through their word), He said, "And the glory which Thou gavest me I have given them." John 17:5, 22. So that glory is ours now, if we will but have it.

When Christ came to this earth His real nature did not appear to the most of those who saw Him. To them He was only an ordinary man. "He came unto His own, and His own received him no." John 1:11. Yet He was the Son of God. Even so it is with those who through Him have received the adoption. "Behold, what manner of love the Father hath bestowed upon us, that we should be called the sons of God: therefore the world knoweth us not, because it knew Him not. Beloved, now are we the sons of God, and it doth not yet appear what we shall be: but we know that, when He shall appear, we shall be like Him; for we shall see Him as He is." 1 John 3:1-2.

With this agree the words of the Apostle Paul: "For our conversation [citizenship] is in heaven; from whence also we look for the Saviour, the Lord Jesus Christ: who shall change our vile body, that it may be fashioned like unto his glorious body, according to the working whereby He is able even to subdue all things unto Himself." Philippians 3:20-21.

Remember that Christ says He has given to His disciples the glory that the Father has given Him. That glory was once seen upon Christ, when the three disciples were with Him in the Mount of Transfiguration. That same glory will be ours when He comes, although it does not yet appear. The brightness of His glory was veiled when he was on earth, and so it is in those in whom He dwells. But it is there nevertheless, only waiting the coming of the Lord to be revealed. And the apostle again says, "The Spirit itself beareth witness with our spirit, that we are the children of God: and if children, then heirs; heirs of God and joint-heirs with Christ; if so be that we suffer with Him, that we may be also glorified together. For I reckon that the sufferings of this present time are not worthy to be compared with the glory which shall be revealed in us." Romans 8:16-18. Mark, the glory is to be revealed in us. The glory will have been there all the time in the shape of the grace of God, and when He shall appear it will be revealed.

This also appears in these word: "Having predestinated us unto the adoption of children by Jesus Christ to Himself, according to the good pleasure of His Will, to the praise of the glory of his grace, wherein He hath made us accepted in the Beloved." Ephesians 1:5-6. So the grace of the Lord has glory. It is glory.

But the interchangeability, or rather the identity of grace and glory, are further shown in these words: "God, who is rich in mercy, for His great love wherewith He loved us, even when we were dead in sins, hath quickened us together with Christ (by grace ye are saved): and hath raised us up together, and made us sit together in heavenly places in Christ Jesus: that in the ages to come He might shew the exceeding riches of His grace in His kindness toward us through Christ Jesus." Ephesians 2:4-7.

That is, just as in this present time the glory of God is given to us in the shape of grace - grace according to the riches of His glory - so that we may be to the praise of the glory of His grace; even so in the ages to come, when the righteous shall "shine forth as the sun in the kingdom of their Father," (Matthew 13:43) "the brightness of the firmament," (Daniel 12:3) with which they will be clothed, will only show forth the riches of His grace by which they were saved. The glory of the stars, in which they will shine forever and ever, will be but the flashing forth of the grace with which, in their mortal life, they were filled by the indwelling of Christ.

Note still further. We have learned that the goodness of God is His Glory, and that it is with His goodness that he clothes us. Now read the further evidence that we, in this present time, receive glory from god. "But we all, with unveiled face reflecting as a mirror the glory of the Lord, are transformed into the same image from glory to glory, even as from the lord the Spirit." 2 Corinthians 3:18.

The allusion is here to the face of Moses when he was conveying the word of God to the people. He talked with God face to face as a man with his friend, and his own face became glorified by the glory from the face of God. Thus we are to reflect the glory of God. But as Moses "wist not that the skin of his face shone," Exodus 34:29 so the one who is progressing from glory to glory in the light of the Lord will himself be unconscious of the transformation.

In view of the transforming power of the glory of God, how rich is the blessing pronounced upon the children of Israel, "The Lord bless thee, and keep thee: The Lord make His face shine upon thee, and be gracious unto thee: the Lord lift up His countenance upon thee, and give thee peace." Numbers 6:24-26.

Therefore, "Blessed is the people that know the joyful sound: they shall walk, O Lord, in the light of Thy countenance. In Thy name shall they rejoice all the day: and in Thy righteousness shall they be exalted. For thou art the glory of their strength." Psalms 89:15-17.

"Lord, Thy glory fills the heaven;

Earth is with its goodness stored;

Unto thee be glory given,

Holy, holy, holy Lord!

Heaven is still with anthems ringing;

Earth takes up the angels' cry,

Holy, holy, holy, singing,

Lord of hosts, Thou Lord Most High."

"Jesus, Hail! Whose glory brightens

All above, and gives it worth;

Lord of life, Thy smile enlightens,

Cheers and charms Thy saints on earth;

When we think of love like Thine,

Lord, we own it love Divine.

Hallelujah! Hallelujah!

Hallelujah! Amen.

"King of glory, reign for ever,

Thine an everlasting crown;

Nothing from thy love shall sever

Those whom Thou shalt call Thine own;

Happy objects of Thy grace,

Destined to behold Thy face!

Hallelujah! Hallelujah!

Hallelujah! Amen.

"Saviour, hasten Thine appearing;

Bring, O bring, the glorious day,

When, the awful summons hearing,

Heaven and earth shall pass away!

Then with golden harps we'll sing,

Glory, glory to our King!

Hallelujah! Hallelujah!

Hallelujah! Amen."

Chapter 5—The Fifth Day

Birds, fishes and beasts

"And God said, Let the waters bring forth abundantly the moving creature that hath life, and fowl that may fly above the earth in the open firmament of heaven.... And God said, "Let the earth bring forth the living creature after his kind, cattle, and creeping thing, and beast of the earth his kind": and it was so. And God made the best of the earth after his kind, and cattle after their kind, and every thing that creepeth upon the earth after his kind: and God saw that it was good." Genesis 1:20, 24-25.

All this was written for our learning. From the living creatures around us, as well as from inanimate nature, God designs that we shall learn lessons concerning Him and His love.

"But ask now the beasts, and they shall teach thee;

And the fowls of the air, and they shall tell thee:

Or speak to the earth, and it shall teach thee:

And the fishes of the sea shall declare unto thee.

Who knoweth not in all these

That the hand of the lord hath wrought this?

In whose hand is the soul of every living thing,

And the breath of all mankind." Job 12.7-10.

The great lesson that we are to learn from the lower orders of creation is the care that God cares for the lowest; He has made in His own image, and places over the works of His hands. The Saviour said, "Are not two sparrows sold for a farthing? And one of them shall not fall on the ground without your Father." Matthew 10.29. Still stronger: "Are not five sparrows sold for two farthings, and not one of them is forgotten before God? But even the very hairs of your head are all numbered. Fear not therefore: ye are of more value than many sparrows." Luke 12:6-7.

Again the Lord says, "Behold the fowls of the air: for they sow not, neither do they reap, nor gather into barns: yet your Heavenly Father feeds them. Are ye not much better than they?" Matthew 6:26. In the care of God for the birds we have the assurance that He will care for us; and as they do not spend time in anxious thought and worry, much less need we. Surely God will take as much better care of men than He does of birds, as the needs and the value of men are greater than those of the birds.

But the care of God for the birds does more than assure us of His care for our physical wants. The life is more than meat. God's care assures us that He will supply all our need, "according to His riches in glory." Philippians 4:19. He, who cares for that which is least, will not forget that which is the greatest. We should take God's care for the wants of the smallest of His creatures as comfort when we appear before the throne of grace to ask for mercy, and grace to help in time of need. Here is our warrant: -

"The Lord is gracious, and full of compassion;

Slow to anger, and of great mercy.

The Lord is good to all;

And Lord is good to all;

And His tender mercies are over all His works.

All Thy works shall give thanks unto Thee, O Lord;

And Thy saints shall bless Thee.

They shall speak of the glory of Thy kingdom,

And talk of thy power;

To make known to the sons of men His mighty acts,

And the glory of the majesty of His kingdom.

Thy kingdom is everlasting kingdom,

And Thy dominion endureth throughout all generations.

The Lord upholdeth all that fall,

And raiseth up all those that be bowed down.

The eyes of all wait upon Thee;

And Thou givest them their meat in due season.

> Thou openest Thine hand,
>
> And satisfieth the desire of every living thing.
>
> The Lord is righteous in all His ways,
>
> And gracious in all His works.
>
> The Lord is nigh unto all them that call upon Him,
>
> To all that call upon Him in truth.
>
> He will fulfill the desire of them that fear Him;
>
> He also will hear their cry, and will save them."
>
> Psalms 145:8-19, R.V.

But the fact that God cares for all His creatures, and that all get their supplies from His open hand, does not imply that they are to sit still and wait for the food to drop into their mouths. He provides food for all, and expects them to take it.

> "These wait all upon Thee,
>
> That Thou mayest give them their meat in due season.
>
> That Thou givest unto them they gather;
>
> Thou openest Thine hand, they are satisfied with good."
>
> Psalms 104:27-28, R.V.

The birds fly about, and gather that which the Lord has provided for them; but that does not indicate that they do not receive it direct from the hand of God. So the fact that man works for his living is no sign that he does not receive it direct from the Lord. Man is actually as much dependent on the lord for his daily bread as the birds are for their food. But for God's provident care there would be nothing to gather, and but for the same care there would be no ability on the part of man to gather it. "When thou hast eaten and art full, then thou shalt bless the Lord thy God for the good land which He hath given thee. Beware that thou forget not the Lord thy God, In not keeping his commandments, and His judgments, and His statutes, which I command thee this day: lest when thou hast eaten and art full, and hast built goodly houses, and dwelt therein; then thine heart be lifted up, and thou forget the Lord thy God,...and thou say in thine heart, my power and the might of mine hand hath gotten me this wealth. But thou shalt remember the Lord thy God: for it is He that giveth thee power to get wealth." Deuteronomy 8:10-18.

From the physical we are to learn lessons concerning the spiritual. God has provided every spiritual blessing that man needs, and more than he can realize. "Blessed be the God and Father of our Lord Jesus Christ, who hath blessed us with all spiritual blessings in heavenly places [things] in Christ." Ephesians 1:3. A man to whom this was quoted once asked, "If this is so, why do I not have all spiritual blessings? Why is it that I lack so much, and have so little enjoyment in the Christian life?' The answer ran thus: "What would you say of a man who should come to your house nearly starved, if, when you had loaded the table with the best that your house affords, he still wrings his hands, and moans, 'Oh, I am so hungry; how I wish I had something to eat!' You would say, that if he is hungry the fault is all his own; that plenty has been given him, and that all he has to do is to take hold and eat. The fact that he is still starving does not prove that you have not given him everything he needs. Thus it is with the gracious gifts of God. He has given you all spiritual blessings, and if you lack it is because you will not take that which He has so richly provided."

The man insisted that this was not a fair illustration, for, said he, "the beggar can see the food before him on the table, but I cannot see the blessings of God." True, we cannot see them, but we may be surer of them than if we could see them. We have the assurance of the word of God that they have been given to us, and there can be no doubt about it. Our eyes often deceive us, but the word of the Lord never does. "The things which are seen are temporal; but the things which are not seen are eternal." 2 Corinthians 4:18. God's word makes things so that did not exist before; therefore we may rest assured that all things that we need for this life, as well as for that which is to come, have been freely given to us, and that we have only to appropriate them.

Chapter 6—The Sixth Day

What is man?

"When I consider Thy heavens, the work of Thy fingers, the moon and the stars, which Thou hast ordained; what is man, that Thou art mindful of him? And the son of man, that Thou visitest him?" Psalms 8:3-4. Thus spoke the Psalmist, and thus must every one feel who has any just sense of the works of God. It is common for men to have a high opinion of themselves and of their merits; so much so that they forget their dependence upon God. It is natural for man to feel independent, and to imagine that he supports himself, and can even continue his own existence.

The drift of men's minds is aptly described by the historian when he says of the ancient philosophers, that in the sublime inquiry concerning human nature "their reason had been often guided by their imagination, and that their imagination had been prompted by their vanity. When they viewed with complacency the extent of their own mental powers; when they exercised the various faculties of memory, of fancy, and of judgment, in the most profound speculations, or the most important labors; and when they reflected upon the desire of fame, which transported them into future ages, far beyond the bounds of death and of the grave, they were unwilling to confound themselves with the beasts of the field, or to suppose that a being for whose dignity they entertained the most sincere admiration could be limited to a spot of earth, and to a few years of duration." ("Decline and Fall," chap. xv., par.18.)

Even so are they described by the Apostle Paul, "Because that, when they knew God, they glorified Him not as God, neither were thankful; but became vain in their imaginations, and their foolish heart was darkened. Professing themselves to be wise, they became fools, and changed the glory of the incorruptible God into an image made like to corruptible man, and to birds, and four footed beasts, and creeping things." Such was their pride and self-conceit that "they did not like to retain God in their knowledge." Romans 1:21-23, 28.

Far different is the disposition of one who is truly wise. King David also carried on some investigations in human nature, but from a different point of view. His desire was to know what God would say of him. "My heart was hot within me, while I was musing the fire burned: then spake I with my tongue, Lord, make me to know mine end, and the measure of my days, what it is: that I may know how frail I am. Behold, Thou hast made my days as an handbreadth; and mine age is as nothing before Thee: verily every man at his best state is altogether vanity." Psalms 39:3-5.

Again, considering the pit which the heathen had made for themselves, and into which they had sunk, and how they were boasting against God, he prayed, "Put them in fear, O Lord: that the nations may know themselves to be but men." Psalms 9:20. Just think of it! "But men!" The nations would make their boast in the fact that they were men, and would consider themselves competent to dispense with God altogether; but God's word says that they are only men. Man is nothing in himself, and can be only as God gives Him opportunity and power.

Let us stop a moment to read what the Scripture says of the origin of man. "And God said, Let us make man in our image, after our likeness: and let them have dominion over the fish of the sea, and over the fowl of the air, and over the cattle, and over all the earth, and over every creeping thing that creepeth upon the earth. So God created man in His own image, in the image of God created He him; male and female created He them." Genesis 1:26-27. "And the Lord God formed man of the dust of the ground, and breathed into his nostrils the breath of life (plural lives); and man became a living soul [living creature]." Genesis 2:7.

Like the beasts, he was taken from the ground. He is but "dust and ashes." He cannot boast at all, not even over the beasts that are placed under him; for it is simply by the power of God, who can make of the same clay a vessel unto honor and one unto dishonor, that he is any different from them. The earth is the source from which all animate creatures spring. "All are of the dust, and all turn to dust again." Ecclesiastes 3:20. After death and decomposition the dust of the prince cannot be distinguished from the dust of the pauper, nor even from that of his dog. If at the last he does not share the fate of the beasts, and go into oblivion, it is only because he has had humility enough to accept the wisdom that comes from God; for "man that is in honor, and understandeth not, is like the beasts that perish." Psalms 49:20. "Oh, why should the spirit of mortal be proud?"

Man is made from the dust, that he may remember that he is nothing in himself; but also in the image of God, that he may know the infinite possibilities before him - association with God Himself; of himself having no more might than the dust upon which he walks, but capable of the greatest things through the power and goodness of God. And, strange as it may seem, his capabilities are the greatest when he is most sensible of his weakness. "When I am weak, then am I strong." 2 Corinthians 12:10.

"And the Lord God formed man of the dust of the ground, and breathed into his nostrils the breath of life; and man became a living soul." Genesis 2:7. Not even here can men claim superiority. The beasts of the field breathe the same air that he does. It is also to them, the same as to him, the gift of God. Indeed, the very fact that his breath is in his nostrils is a proof of his frailty. "Cease yourselves from such a man, whose breath is in his nostrils: for of what account is he?" Isaiah 2:22. It is the breath of life, which God has given him, but how feeble a hold he has of it. "For what is your life? It is even a vapor, that appears for a little time, and then vanishes away." James 4:14.

How can this be, since the life was given him from God? It is not that life from God is a slight thing, but because man has so slight a tenure of it. In the hand of God is the breath of every living thing, and at His pleasure He can take it to Himself. "If He set His heart upon man, if He gather unto Himself his spirit and his breath: all flesh shall perish together, and man shall turn again unto dust." Job 34:14-15. "Then shall the dust return to the earth as it was: and the spirit shall return unto God who gave it." Ecclesiastes 12:7. Not yet have we found anything in which man can boast.

How natural it is for men in extremity to turn for help to some other man, or to human power. And yet no man on earth has the power to make any change in his own physical condition. He cannot change the color of his hair, nor add an inch to his stature. "They that trust in their wealth, and boast themselves in the multitude of their riches: none of them can by any means redeem his brother, nor give to God a ransom for him." Psalms 49:6-7. Therefore the exhortation comes, "Put not your trust in princes, nor in the son of man, in whom there is no help. His breath goes forth, he returns to his earth; in that very day his thoughts perish." Psalm 146:3-4. Whom should he trust? "Happy is he that hath the God of Jacob for his help, whose hope is in the Lord his God: which made heaven, and earth, the sea, and all that therein is: which keepeth truth for ever." Psalm 146:5-6.

There is no life but from God. "For with You is the fountain of life." Psalms 36:9. But life is righteousness; "for to be carnally minded is death; but to be spiritually minded is life and peace." Romans 8:6. Sin is death, and is from Satan, and the Son of God was manifested, that He might destroy the works of the devil. Sin is at last to be utterly blotted from the universe, and of necessity those whose lives are still sin must be blotted out with it. If they cling to their sinful lives they must be destroyed with sin. Christ is the righteousness of God; for God alone is good, and in Christ is all the fullness of God. Therefore only those who have Christ can have any hope of life hereafter. In fact, they have no real life now. "This is the record, that God hath given to us eternal life, and this life is in His Son. He that hath the Son hath life; and he that hath not the Son of God hath not life." 1 John 5:11-12. Nay, more than this: "He that believeth not the Son shall not see life." John 3:36

It is true that there will be a resurrection of the dead, both of the just and unjust, but only the righteous will be raised to life; they that have done evil come forth from their graves to the resurrection of damnation. John 5:28-29. Their lot will be to "be punished with everlasting destruction from the presence of the Lord, and from the glory of His power." 2 Thessalonians 1:9. Since they have not the righteousness, which alone is life, there is nothing by which their existence can be continued.

All this is to teach men that there is hope only in God; that He is supreme, and that power belongs alone to Him. Not only a single man, but "all nations before Him are as nothing; and they are counted to Him less than nothing; and vanity." Isaiah 40:17. But while this should make man humble, it should in no wise discourage him. Indeed, it is for our encouragement, for God made the universe from nothing, and so He can take the man who trusts Him, and make of him what He will. To the end "that no flesh should glory in His presence. But of Him are ye in Christ Jesus, who of God is made unto us wisdom, and righteousness, and sanctification, and redemption: that, according as it is written, He that glories, let him glory in the Lord." 1 Corinthians 1:29-31. Surely man should not be ashamed to acknowledge his lowly origin, since through Christ he may do all things.

One more lesson of encouragement may be learned from the frailty of man, which shows that only in humility is true exaltation found. Since all things come from God, man can be at his highest state only when he gladly acknowledges that he is nothing, and yields to the loving power of God. The fortieth chapter of Isaiah contains the message, which is to prepare a people for the coming of the Lord in glory. It is a message of comfort, because it tells of the power of God. Here is the message: -

"The voice of him that cries in the wilderness, Prepare ye the way of the Lord, make straight in the desert a highway for our God. Every valley shall be exalted, and every mountain and hill shall be made low: and the crooked shall be made straight, and the rough places plain: and the glory of the Lord shall be revealed and all flesh shall see it together: for the mouth of the Lord hath spoken it. The voice said, Cry. And he said, what shall I cry? All flesh is grass, and all the goodliness thereof is as the flower of the field: the grass withers, the flower fades: because the Spirit of the Lord bloweth upon it: surely the people is grass. The grass withers, the flower fades: but the word of our God shall stand for ever." Isaiah 40:1-8.

That which is to prepare men for the glorious appearing of our Lord and Saviour Jesus Christ, when He comes to reward every man according as his work shall be, is the full acceptance of the message that man is nothing, and that God is everything. His alone is the power, and His word works effectually in every one that believeth. The works that will stand the test of the judgment are the works that are wrought in God. "All flesh is grass"; but we have seen how the power of God is most wonderfully shown in the grass. It was the word of God that said, "Let the earth bring forth grass," and that is the word which liveth and abideth forever, and which is by the Gospel preached unto us. We have seen how the power of that word causes the tiny blade of grass to push its way to the surface and the light, in spite of the heavy clods that would hold it down. Infinite power is exhibited in the frail thing. Even so does the word of power work in those who heartily believe it. He who acknowledges himself to be nothing - frail and helpless as the grass - will be strengthened to do mighty deeds, and will be lifted above the clods of earth, into the sunlight of the presence of God.

Chapter 7—The Seventh Day

Resting with the Lord

"Thus the heavens and the earth were finished, and all the host of them. And on the seventh day God ended his work which He had had made; and He rested on the seventh day from all His work which He had made. And God blessed the seventh day, and sanctified it: because that in it He had rested from all His work which God created and made." Genesis 2:1-3.

"Remember the Sabbath day, to keep it holy. Six days shalt thou labor, and do all thy work: but the seventh day is the Sabbath of the Lord thy God: in it thou shalt not do any work, thou, nor thy son, nor thy daughter, thy manservant, nor thy maidservant, nor thy cattle, nor thy stranger that is within thy gates: for in six days the Lord made heaven and earth, the sea, and all that in them is, and rested the seventh day: wherefore the Lord blessed the Sabbath day, and hallowed it." Exodus 20:8-11.

This is the grand summary of creation, and the account of the celebration of it. The days of creation are sufficiently designated by being numbered, but the day that completes (and celebrates) creation is honored by having a name. The name of the seventh day is "Sabbath." Thus a double purpose is served. By the naming of the seventh day it is distinguished from all other days, and by the numbering of the others without naming them the fact that the Sabbath is a definitely recurring day is made prominent. But the text tells its own story as to the day, which is the Sabbath; and it is one of the sure commandments of God, which "stand fast for ever and ever." Psalms 111:8. What we are to do here is to call attention to the spiritual lessons to be learned from the giving of the Sabbath to man.

Christ is the great Creator. He is the wisdom of God, and the power of God. "For in Him were all things created, in the heavens and upon the earth, things visible and things invisible, whether thrones or dominions, or principalities or powers; all things have been created through Him, and unto Him; and He is before all things, and in Him all things consist." Colossians 1:16, 17, R.V

"Without Him was not anything made that was made." John 1:3. When the record says that in six days God made the heavens and the earth, it means God in Christ, for Christ is the only manifestation of God that is known to men. Therefore, also, we know that it must have been Christ who rested upon the seventh day, after completing the work of creation, and that is was Christ who blessed the seventh day and sanctified it. Thus the Sabbath day is in an emphatic sense the "Lord's Day."

Why was the Sabbath made? "The Sabbath was made for man." Mark 2:27. It is for him, in the sense that is not against him. It is not an arbitrary thing imposed upon man, something for him to keep simply because God says so, - but something that is given him for his help. It is a blessing that God has bestowed upon him. It is among the "all things that pertain unto life and godliness," 2 Peter 1:3 which His Divine power has given unto us.

Why was the Sabbath given? The Lord, through the prophet, gives the answer in these words: "And hallow My Sabbaths; and they shall be a sign between Me and you, that ye may know that I am the Lord your God." Ezekiel 20:20. Mark, it is a sign by which the people are to know God. Therefore there is no room for the supposition that the Sabbath was simply for the purpose of distinguishing the Jews from other people. It was made before the Jews had any existence. It was that they might know God; and that which would serve to make them know God, would serve the same purpose for all other people. It was given to Adam in the beginning for the same purpose, - that He might know and remember God.

But how would the Sabbath be a sign that men might know God? The answer to this is found in the Epistle to the Romans: "Because that which may be known of God is manifest in them; for God hath shewed it unto them. For the invisible things of Him from [or, ever since] the creation of the world are clearly seen, being understood by the things that are made, even His eternal power and Godhead; so that they are without excuse." Romans 1:19-20. We have only to recall some of the things noted in the preceding pages to see how God is known by His works.

Yet again the question comes, "How does the Sabbath make us know the true God?" Why, we have just read that the eternal power and Godhead of the Creator are seen from the things that He has made; and the Sabbath is the great memorial of creation. The Lord rested upon the seventh day, after the six days of creation, and He blessed and sanctified the day, because that in it He had rested from all his words. So we read, "The works of the Lord are great, sought out of all them that have pleasure therein. His work is honorable and glorious: and His righteousness endureth forever. He hath made His wonderful works to be remembered: the Lord is gracious and full of compassion". Some versions give, more literally, "He hath made a memorial for His wonderful works." Psalms 111:2-4.

The one thing necessary for man to learn in this life is God. The poet may tell us that the proper study of mankind is God. "Thus saith the Lord, Let not the wise man glory in his wisdom, neither let the mighty man glory in his might, let not the rich man glory in his riches: but let him that glories glory in this, that he understandeth and knoweth Me, that I am the Lord which exercise loving-kindness, judgment, and righteousness, in the earth: for in these things I delight, saith the Lord." Jeremiah 9:23-24. Knowing Him, we have all that is worth knowing, for He is the truth, and all the truth. Jesus Christ is the wisdom of God, and in Him are contained "all the treasures of wisdom and knowledge." Colossians 2:3.

The Sabbath is for the purpose of keeping in mind the creative power of God, which is His distinguishing characteristic. But creative power is the power of the Gospel, so that that which celebrates creation also celebrates redemption. Christ is the Redeemer, because in Him were all things created. He bestows the grace of God to men by His creative power. The power that saves men is the power that created the heavens and the earth. So when the Psalmist says that the Lord has made a memorial for His wonderful works, he immediately adds, "The Lord is gracious and full of compassion." In Christ the grace of the Father is revealed. "And the Word was made flesh and dwelt among us (and we beheld His glory, the glory as of the only begotten of the Father), full of grace and truth." John 1:14. He imparts His grace, which affords help in time of need, by the same mysterious and mighty power by which He created the earth; by the same power by which the sun's rays impart life to the plants on the earth.

Note how inseparably Christ is connected with the Sabbath. It is by Him that all things were created, and that they all are upheld. But the works of God reveal His eternal power and Godhead; and Christ is the power of God, and in him dwells all the fullness of the Godhead bodily. Therefore the works of creation show the power and Divinity of the Lord Jesus Christ. The Sabbath is the great memorial of the wonderful works of God in Christ, and so it is the great sign of the Divinity of Christ. To keep the Sabbath as God appointed it at creation is to acknowledge the Divinity of Christ. Just to the extent that one fails to keep the Sabbath of the Lord in spirit and in truth, does he fail to recognize the Divinity of Christ, and to receive the benefit that comes from the fact of His Divinity.

This is indicated in the words of Christ to the Pharisees who unjustly accused Him and His disciples of breaking the Sabbath, because they satisfied their hunger on that day, and because He healed a man on the Sabbath. Said He, "The Son of man is Lord even of the Sabbath day." Matthew 12:8. It is no small thing that He is Lord of the Sabbath day. To be Lord of the Sabbath day means that He is the Creator of the heavens and the earth - that He is Lord of all.

There is a special blessing connected with the Sabbath. It is true that very many who profess to keep the Sabbath do not receive that blessing; but that is because they do not really know of it. The statement of the Scripture is, that God blessed the seventh day, and hallowed it. He blessed the day. There is no day of the week when the Lord may not bless men. Indeed, both good and bad are alike the subjects of the blessings of God every day. Not only so, but those who seek the Lord may find special blessings at any time. The Lord is always near at hand, and lies always ready to bless; but there is a blessing that goes with the Sabbath day that cannot be found anywhere else. It is the Sabbath blessing. God has put His blessing upon the Sabbath, and the Sabbath blessing goes only with the Sabbath. Nobody can find a thing where it is not. The Sabbath blessing has not been placed upon any day except the seventh; therefore it cannot be found anywhere else.

What is this blessing for? It is for the same purpose that all the blessings of God are given. "Unto you first God, having raised up His Son Jesus, sent Him to bless you, in turning away every one of you from his iniquities." Acts 3:26. God blesses men, not because they are good, but in order that they may become good. All His blessings are for the purpose of turning them away from sin to Himself. If men do know the Lord, then the blessings that He bestows are for the purpose of drawing them still closer to Him. So it is with the Sabbath. It is to turn men to God, by reminding them of His goodness and of His gracious power. The power of creation is the power of Christ. Christ is of God, "made unto us wisdom, and righteousness, and sanctification, and redemption." The power by which He gives us these things is the power by which He created the worlds. Therefore we find a deeper meaning in the words of the Lord, "Moreover also I gave them My Sabbaths, to be a sign between Me and them, that they might know that I am the Lord that sanctify them." Ezekiel 20:12. The blessing of the Sabbath is the blessing of sanctification. As the Sabbath is the memorial of God's creation, so is it to make known to us the power of God, to make us entirely new creatures in Christ.

The word "Sabbath" means rest. It is the untranslated Hebrew word signifying rest. So where we read, "The seventh day is the Sabbath of the Lord thy God", it is the same as though it read, "The seventh day is the rest of the Lord thy God." That this is so will be plain to any one who recalls the statement that on the seventh day God rested from all His works, which He had made.

Now let it be remembered that it is the Sabbath of the Lord that we are called upon to keep. In these days we hear such terms as "The Jewish Sabbath," "The Continental Sabbath," "The Puritan Sabbath," "The American Sabbath," "The Christians' Sabbath," etc.; but the only Sabbath that the Bible tells of is "The Sabbath of the Lord thy God." "Verily My Sabbaths ye shall keep." Exodus 31:13. The Lord speaks of the Sabbath as "My holy day." Isaiah 58:13. Therefore it is the Lord's rest that we are to keep. Not merely are we to abstain from our own work on the day on which the Lord rested, but we are to keep His rest. What does this mean? Let us see.

The Saviour tells us "God is a Spirit." John 4:24. More exact is the marginal reading of the Revised Version, "God is Spirit." He is not merely one of a number of spirits, but He is Spirit. He is a spiritual, not a physical, Being. Does that mean that He is only a shadow? Not by any means. The only enduring things are those that are spiritual. God is substance, for it is declared that Christ is "the very image of His substance." Hebrews 1:3, R.V.

It is a mistaken idea that we are so prone to get, that spiritual things are unreal. "There is a natural body, and there is a spiritual body." 1 Corinthians 15:44. Christ's body after His resurrection, the body with which He ascended to heaven, was certainly a spiritual body; yet it was very real and tangible. We cannot tell what a spiritual body is, but we know that it is infinitely higher and more perfect than our physical bodies. It is not subject to the limitations that natural, physical bodies are.

God is Spirit; therefore the rest that He took after creation was spiritual rest. There was no physical weariness incurred in creating the earth. "The everlasting God, the Lord, the Creator of the ends of the earth, fainteth not, neither is weary." Isaiah 40:28. Creation was not a physical work; it was wholly spiritual. God spake, and it was. And His word is spirit. Therefore, to keep God's Sabbath, or rest, is to enjoy spiritual rest. The Sabbath is not designed for mere physical rest, but for spiritual. It has a higher meaning than is commonly attached to it. True, we are enjoined from doing our own labor on that day, but the cessation from physical labor on the Sabbath day is but an emblem of the spiritual rest which God gives to those who accept Him as the Creator of all things. Without spiritual rest there is no true Sabbath-keeping. The Lord says, that they who turn away their feet from the Sabbath, and do not do their own ways on His holy day, but call the Sabbath a delight, the holy of the Lord, honorable, shall delight themselves in the Lord. Isaiah 58:13-14. A man may refrain from labor on the seventh day as scrupulously as ever the strictest Pharisee did; yet if he does not know and delight in the Lord Jesus Christ, he is not keeping the Sabbath of the Lord. True Sabbath rest can be found only in Christ.

Let it not be forgotten, that the Sabbath was given to man in Eden before sin entered into the world. Work was given to Adam, but it was not wearisome labor. Labor is no part of the curse, but weariness from labor is. It was not until after the fall that it was said to Adam, "Cursed is the ground for thy sake; in sorrow shalt thou eat of it all the days of thy life; thorns also and thistles shall it bring forth to thee; and thou shalt eat the herb of the field; in the sweat of thy face shalt thou eat bread, till thou return unto the ground; for out of it wast thou taken: for dust thou art, and unto dust shalt thou return." Genesis 3:17-19 All this was because he had sinned. If he had remained loyal to God the earth would have yielded bountifully only that which is good, and labor would have been a pleasure. Yet the Sabbath would have been observed, not as a rest for the body, which would never have become weary, but as a season of delightful communion with God.

A practical lesson may be learned right here in regard to Sabbath legislation. If the Sabbath were merely for the purpose of giving men physical rest, in order that they might be able to begin the next week's pursuit of wealth the more eagerly, it would be possible for the Government to require all men to keep the Sabbath. But since the rest of the Sabbath is a spiritual rest, the impossibility of compelling anybody to keep the Sabbath must be apparent. Spiritual pertains to the Spirit of God. The rest of the Sabbath, being spiritual, is the rest, which only the Spirit of God can give, and the Spirit of God is not subject to acts of Parliament, or the decrees of courts. Even though the seventh day, the day, which the Lord Himself blessed and sanctified, were the day, sought to be enforced, the result would be the same. God does not use compulsion, and He has not authorized any man or body of men to use it in His place. The Sabbath is for man; it is the greatest blessing that God has for man. It is that which shows him the power by which he may be saved. To compel men, therefore, to keep the Sabbath, would be the same as to compel them to be saved. Christ says that He will draw men to Him, but He does not drive them. He is the Good Shepherd; as such He goes before His sheep, and leads them by His voice, but He does not drive them with a club.

It is clear that mere bodily recuperation is not the object of the Sabbath day, and that merely refraining from bodily toil does not at all constitute the sum of Sabbath-keeping. Yet entire cessation of our own work, of whatever kind it may be, is enjoined on the seventh day. This not alone for the purpose of giving us time to contemplate the works of God without interruption, but to impress a much needed lesson of trust in God. As we cease all our labor by which we earn our living, we are reminded of the fact that God supplies us not only with spiritual blessings, but also with all temporal necessities.

We thereby acknowledge that although, in obedience to His command, we labor for our daily bread, we are as dependent upon Him as though we did nothing.

A proper understanding of the Sabbath and its object, therefore, would for ever set at rest the inquiry that often arises in the minds of persons who are convinced that they ought to obey God in the matter of Sabbath observance. The question is, "If I should keep the seventh day, how could I make a living? I shall doubtless lose my position, and since but comparatively few people keep that day, and it is the principal business day of the week, I shall not be able to find employment. What can I do?" I say one who knows the nature and object of the Sabbath will never ask such a question. He will know that the Sabbath itself points out the answer. The very idea of Sabbath observance is that of perfect trust in God, whose power brought the universe from nothing, and upholds it, and whose love for His creatures is equal to His power to do them good.

It will also solve the question, or rather, prevent its arising, as to whether a man should in an extremity labor on the Sabbath in harvest, when that seems to be the only hope of securing the crop. He will know that the God who alone can make the corn grow, is fully able to protect it, or to make ample provision for him in another way if it should be destroyed. But all will understand that perfect Sabbath-keeping is consistent with bestowing all needful care upon the afflicted; for the Sabbath itself reminds us that God is "gracious and full of compassion."

"Let us therefore fear, lest, a promise being left us of entering into His rest, any of you should seem to come short of it. For unto us was the Gospel preached, as well as unto them (the Jews): but the word preached did not profit them, not being mixed with faith in them that heard it. For we, which have believed, do enter into rest, as He said, As I have sworn in My wrath, if they shall enter (they shall not enter) into My rest: although the works were finished from the foundation of the world. For He spake in a certain place of the seventh day on this wise, And God did rest the seventh day from all His works.... There remaineth therefore a rest to the people of God. For he that is entered into His rest, He also hath ceased from His own works, as God did from His." Hebrews 4:1-10.

The rest that is here spoken of is evidently the rest that remains for the people of God in the everlasting kingdom of our Lord and Saviour Jesus Christ. It is rest in the earth made new, which the ancient Jews did not obtain because of unbelief. That which they received in the land of Canaan was only a shadow of the real rest, which God had promised them. The same Gospel of the kingdom, which is preached to us, was first preached to them. But what has the seventh day to do with that eternal rest in the kingdom of God? We shall see.

The Sabbath is the memorial of creation, as we have seen. But let it not be forgotten that the Sabbath was given at the time when "God saw all that He had made; and behold, it was very good." So the Sabbath commemorates a perfect creation. It reminds us that the earth was not always in the condition in which we now see it. Then, since no word of God can fail, and every purpose will be carried out, just as surely as the Sabbath reminds us of a perfect creation completed for the dwelling-place of man, it assures us that the earth will be renewed, and made fit for the dwelling-place of those who shall be made meet for the inheritance of the saints in light.

"They shall go to confusion together that are makers of idols. But Israel shall be saved in the Lord with an everlasting salvation: ye shall not be ashamed nor confounded world without end. For thus saith the Lord that created the heavens; God Himself that formed the earth and made it; He hath established it, He created it not in vain, He formed it to be inhabited: I am the Lord; and there is none else." Isaiah 14:16-18.

God made the earth, and placed man upon it. When man was created he was upright; therefore God intended the earth to be inhabited by a race of perfect beings. To these beings He gave the Sabbath, that they might keep in mind their Creator, and thus retain their perfection. That perfection was not merely physical perfection, but it was spiritual as well. Man, in perfection of character, was made in the image of God. So he was to observe the Sabbath, as a reminder of the spiritual perfection that he had received from God, and that could be preserved by Him alone. Now it is to that perfect condition that the Lord is going to restore the earth, and through the Gospel He is preparing a perfect people to inhabit the restored earth. Although man has fallen, and the earth has been defiled, the Sabbath still remains, a fragment of Eden, both as a reminder to man of what God prepared in the beginning, and as a means of lifting him up to that high position, so that he may enjoy it when it is restored.

The rest that remains, therefore, is the earth renewed and Eden restored. The works were finished from the foundation of the world. That is, as soon as the earth was created it was man's rest. Man was given work to do, but it was not wearisome work. A strictly literal rendering of Genesis 2:15 would be, that God caused man to rest in the garden, which He had planted. He gave man rest in the earth that was ready for his enjoyment. The proof of this is found in the words, "And God did rest the seventh day from all His works." Then the Sabbath was given to man as a sign that he was to rest to all eternity with the Lord. That is, he was to enjoy spiritual rest, - perfect freedom from all sin.

During the six days God had been speaking the words that brought the earth to its perfect condition. Then He rested. He ceased speaking, and His word, which liveth and abideth forever, continued to uphold that which was created. So God rested upon His word. He could rest from the work of creation, in perfect confidence that His word would uphold the universe. So when we keep the Sabbath of the Lord, we simply take the rest that comes from settling down upon the promises of God.

Thus it is that "we which have believed do enter into rest." And he that hath entered into rest, he also hath ceased from his own works, as God did from His. Before men fully accept the simple word of the Lord everything is from self. The works of the flesh are only sin; and even though men profess to serve God, and have earnest desires to do right, their own works to that end are failures. "All our righteousnesses are as filthy rags." Isaiah 64.6. But when we realize the power of the word of God, and know that it is able to build up those who trust it, then we cease our own works, and allow God to work in us, both to will and to do of His good pleasure. Then all our works are wrought in Him, and they are right. This is indeed rest. The rest that comes when we realize that salvation does not come from ourselves, but from the word which made the heavens and the earth, and which upholds them, is the rest which the Sabbath brings to us when it is kept as the Lord designs.

Notice that we are to remember the Sabbath day, to keep it holy. It is holy, and so we are to keep it. We are not to make it holy, for that would be impossible; only God could do that. No act of ours can add to or detract from its holiness. Neither are we to make ourselves holy, so that we may keep it properly. That we could not do. But the same power that sanctified the Sabbath day will sanctify us. That power is the power that made the universe. It is creative power by which we are to be sanctified, for Christ is the Creator, and He is made unto us wisdom, and righteousness, and sanctification, and redemption. God has given us the Sabbath, - the memorial of His creative power, - that we may know that He is the God that sanctifies us.

This is the rest that Christ gives to all that come to Him. He says, "Come unto Me, all ye that labor and are heavy laden, and I will give you rest. Take My yoke upon you, and learn of Me; for I am meek and lowly in heart: and ye shall find rest unto your souls." Matthew 11:28-29. We are to come and rest upon the word that upholds the universe. This is what the Sabbath means. It commemorates creation; but redemption is simply the power that created all things, working to restore them. So the Sabbath marks the highest Gospel attainments.

We have seen that the Sabbath was given in Eden, and that it is a part of that rest upon which God entered. When kept in spirit and in truth, it is a bit of Eden preserved for us, through all the changes wrought by the curse. And as God made not the earth in vain, but formed it to be inhabited by the same class of people whom He first placed upon it, so it will yet be. Therefore the Sabbath is not only a portion of the original Eden preserved for us, but it is also identical with that rest that will be enjoyed by the saints of God throughout eternity. Heaven does indeed begin upon earth for those who fully accept the Saviour, and who give themselves to Him without reserve. The Sabbath - a fragment of Paradise - spans the chasm from Eden lost till Eden restored, and, as it is the memorial of the first, it is the pledge of the second.

Is not the Sabbath, then, indeed a delight? Can any one who understands what it means regard it in any other light than a blessing? The man of God has given us a song for the Sabbath day, in which he shows how it is to be regarded, and what it is to do for us. "It is a good thing to give thanks unto the Lord, and to sing praises unto Thy name, O Most High: to show forth Thy faithfulness every night, upon an instrument of ten strings, and upon the psaltery; upon the harp with a solemn sound. For Thou, Lord, hast made me glad through Thy hands." Psalms 92:1-4. We are to be strong in the Lord, and in the power of His might. We are to be overcomers "through Him that loved us." So when we are beset with temptation, we have only to think of the power of God, - the power that made the worlds from nothing, - and know that it will be put forth for our deliverance if we will but accept it. Nothing is too hard for the Lord, and there is nothing able to withstand Him. All the hosts of Satan have no power when engaged in a contest with the Lord. Christ has "spoiled principalities and powers." Colossians 2:15. So when we rest ourselves on that power, the victory is already won. The things that God has made remind us of His power, and so we triumph in the works of His hands. This glorious victory is what the Sabbath is intended to bring to us.

So as the Sabbath is the sign of a perfect creation, it is the seal of a new creature in Christ. It is therefore the seal of God, ministered by the Spirit of God. As it came from Paradise, and is a part of the rest of Paradise, so it shows that those who keep it in spirit (not in form merely) are, through the mighty power of God, destined for a place in Paradise. And thus it will come to pass that, in the ages to come, when Eden is restored, all flesh shall come together from Sabbath to Sabbath to worship.

God, whose love and power and kindness in Christ have brought them to share the glories of His presence. And as they assemble on those thrice-blessed Sabbath days they will sing, "Worthy is the Lamb that was slain to receive power, and riches, and wisdom, and strength, and honor, and glory, and blessing." But the redeemed host will not be alone in their praises. All the works of God praise Him even now, while groaning, and waiting for the redemption; but then, when every trace of the curse will have been removed, and the Gospel has brought back the original creation, "Every creature which is in heaven, and on the earth, and under the earth, and such as are in the sea, and all that are in them," will in perfection unite as with one voice in saying, "Blessing, and honor, and glory, and power, be unto Him that sitteth upon the throne, and unto the Lamb for ever and ever." Revelation 5:12-13.

Otros libros del Autor y del Mensaje de 1888 disponibles:

1. Descubriendo la Cruz, Autor: Robert J. Wieland.

2. Introducción al Mensaje de 1888, Autor: Robert J. Wieland.

3. 1888 Reexaminado, Autores: Robert J. Wieland y Donald K. Short.

4. He aquí, Yo estoy a la Puerta y llamo, Autor: Robert J. Wieland.

5. Diez Grandes Verdades del Evangelio, Autor: Robert J. Wieland.

6. Nuestro Glorioso Futuro, Autor: Robert J. Wieland.

7. Reavivamientos Modernos, Autor: Robert J. Wieland.

8. La Palabra se Hizo Carne, Autor: Ralph Larson.

9. Cristologia en los Escritos de Elena G. de White, Autor: Ralph Larson.

10. El Evangelio en Gálatas, Autor: E. J. Waggoner.

11. Carta a los Romanos, Autor: E. J. Waggoner.

12. El Pacto Eterno, Autor: E. J. Waggoner.

13. Cristo y su Justicia, Autor: E. J. Waggoner.

14. 1888 Materiales; Volúmenes 1-4 en español, Autor: Elena G. de White.

15. El Camino Consagrado a la Perfección Cristiana, Autor: A. T. Jones.

16. El Mensaje del Tercer Ángel; 3 Volúmenes, Autor: A. T. Jones.

17. Lecciones sobre la Fe, Autores: A. T. Jones y E. J. Waggoner.

*Si desea adquirirlos al por mayor (40% descuento), son por cajas de 50 libros (puede ser mixto) y nos puede contactar a este correo:

lsdistribution07@gmail.com

www.ingramcontent.com/pod-product-compliance
Lightning Source LLC
Chambersburg PA
CBHW080900010526
44118CB00015B/2218